Young**Writers** 2005 PO

PLAYGROU

Let your creativity flow...

ode

limerick   haiku

rhyme

ball

Co Antrim Vol I
Edited by Sarah Marshall

 Young**Writers**

First published in Great Britain in 2005 by:
Young Writers
Remus House
Coltsfoot Drive
Peterborough
PE2 9JX
Telephone: 01733 890066
Website: www.youngwriters.co.uk

SB ISBN 1 84602 116 2

Foreword

Young Writers was established in 1991 and has been passionately devoted to the promotion of reading and writing in children and young adults ever since. The quest continues today. Young Writers remains as committed to the fostering of burgeoning poetic and literary talent as ever.

This year's Young Writers competition has proven as vibrant and dynamic as ever and we are delighted to present a showcase of the best poetry from across the UK. Each poem has been carefully selected from a wealth of *Playground Poets* entries before ultimately being published in this, our thirteenth primary school poetry series.

Once again, we have been supremely impressed by the overall high quality of the entries we have received. The imagination, energy and creativity which has gone into each young writer's entry made choosing the best poems a challenging and often difficult but ultimately hugely rewarding task - the general high standard of the work submitted amply vindicating this opportunity to bring their poetry to a larger appreciative audience.

We sincerely hope you are pleased with our final selection and that you will enjoy *Playground Poets Co Antrim Vol I* for many years to come.

Contents

Chloe McGall (10)	37
Caroline Fleck (9)	37
Adam McDowell (11)	38
Sarah Kennedy (10)	38
Amy Hunter (9)	39
Joanne Stirling (9)	39
David Murray (11)	40
Calvin Kernohan (10)	40
Andrew Millar (11)	41
Jak Palmer (10)	41
Shannon Douglas (10)	42
Philip Scroggie (11)	42
Samuel McNabney (11)	43
Christopher Smyth (11)	43
Lee McGavock (11)	44
Jolon Cupples (10)	44
Nathan Houston (11)	45
Catherine McCartney (10)	45
Jenni McCandless (11)	46
Alice McCaughey (10)	46
Stacey McGavock (11)	47
Nicola Galbraith (10)	47
Nicole Bradley (10)	48
Abigail Martin (11)	48
Laura Millar (9)	49
Gary McKendry (11)	49
Samantha Millar (9)	50

Carnaghts Primary School

Katie Hamilton (9)	50
Heather Steele (9)	50
Sarah Wilson (10)	51
Lauren Todd (10)	51
Kathryn McFadden (10)	52
Ruth Gracey (10)	52
Melissa O'Neill (11)	53
Chloe McDonald (10)	53
Shane McBurney (10)	54
Ross Hutchinson (10)	54
Sam Steele (11)	55
Neil Armstrong (10)	55

Creavery Primary School

Jordon Lynn (11)	56
Andrew Warwick (11)	56
Hannah Dennison (11)	57

Groggan Primary School

Rebecca Herbison (9)	57
Rachel Clarke (9)	58
Andrew Rainey (8)	58
Mark McMullen (9)	58
Katherine Aiken (9)	59
Alana Nicholl (10)	59
Danielle Winter (8)	60
Rachael Kenny (8)	60
Leagh Purdy (9)	61
Emma Johnston (9)	61
Kirsty Wallace (8)	62
Carla Cameron (8)	62
Chloe McKee (8)	63
Nicole Cameron (8)	63
Adam Clarke (7)	64
David Speedy (8)	64
Denver Mills (7)	64
Steven Thompson (7)	65
Laura Coulter (7)	65
Thomas Allen (9)	65
Adam McIlmoyle (10)	66
Victoria Graham (9)	66
Kathryn Cameron (11)	67
Sophie Millar (8)	67
Hannah Brown (7)	68
Laura Agnew (8)	68
Rebecca Gregg (10)	69
Michael Craig (8)	69
Amy Wallace (10)	70
Rachel Johnston (11)	70
Shannon Cameron (11)	71
Taylor-Ann Black (11)	71
Ruth McKeown (8)	72
Nicky Black (9)	72
Ileanna McDowell (11)	73

Jonathan McIlroy (9)	73
Stephanie French (11)	73
Philip Smyth (10)	74
Chloe Buick (9)	75
Victoria Bond (10)	75
Andrew Hamill (8)	76

Kilmoyle Primary School

James Freeman (11)	76
Kurtis Ashcroft (10)	77
Sam Kane (11)	77
Naomi Bleakly (9)	78
David Miskelly (11)	78
Laura Freeman (9)	79
James McLaughlin (11)	79
Kris Purdy (10)	80
Charles Stewart (10)	80
Nikita Kane (10)	80
Harry McKeown (9)	81
Nicola Cochrane (10)	81
Elizabeth Morrow (9)	82
Hannah Rose Kirkpatrick (10)	83
Jordan Christie (10)	84

St Comgall's Primary School, Antrim

Ryan McAuley (10)	84
Siobhan McQuillan (11)	85
Ciaran O'Hara (10)	85
Anthony Devlin (11)	86
Matthew Montgomery (11)	86
Shannon Connor (11)	87
Niamh O'Connor (11)	87
Danielle O'Kane (11)	88
Gemma McErlane (10)	88
Chloe Langton (10)	89
Rebecca Kennedy (10)	89
Mollie Somers (11)	90
Alexandra McDonnell (11)	90
Sophie Mahon (10)	91
Natilla Lane (11)	91
Ben Johnston (10)	92

Paul Joyce (10)	92
Dearbháile Liddy (10)	93
Pol McElligott (10)	93
Shannen Dilworth (9)	94
Natasha McMahon (10)	94
Ciara Dilworth (9)	95
Tara Wilson (9)	95
Shannon Close (9)	96
Ciara Devine (10)	96
Dermot Mullin (10)	97
Nathan McGarry (9)	97
Martin Gourley (9)	98
David Quinn (10)	98
Bronagh Lavery (9)	99
Chloe Todd (10)	99
Aaron Geoghegan (10)	99
Lee Mason (9)	100
Callum McAteer (8)	100
Rebecca Moore (9)	100
Karl Thompson (9)	101
Nicole Quinn (9)	101
Gareth Rainey (9)	102
Ryan Bevin (9)	102
Conor Logue (8)	103
Aoife Marley (9)	103
Connor Keenan (8)	104

St Joseph's Primary School, Dunloy

Ruairi McPoland (9)	104
Ryan Kennedy (11)	105
Nicola McShane (10)	105
Catherine McDaid (10)	105
Keelan Harkin (11)	106
Eimer McKendry (8)	106
Megan Kennedy (8)	106
David O'Neill (11)	107
Shauna Draine (11)	107
Annemarie Esler (11)	107
Nicole O'Neill (9)	108
Alastair Dooey (9)	108
Fearghal O'Boyle (8)	108

Stephen McToal (10)	109
Kirstin Ingram (8)	109
Niall Smyth (9)	109
Shannon Carey (9)	110
Leon Dillon (8)	110
Erin Kearns (9)	110
Laura McKeague (10)	111
Thomas McCann (10)	111
Dean Boyle (9)	112
Daniel Henry (9)	112
Morgan Lyttle (9)	112
Blaine McDaid (8)	113
Aisling Crawford (9)	113
Rachael Kearns (9)	113
Aimie Scott (9)	114
Rachel O'Loan (8)	114
Chantelle Smiley (8)	114
Aideen Brogan (11)	115
Ronan Cunning (10)	115
Ronan Martin (10)	115
Caolan McIlfatrick (10)	116
John Kelly (11)	116
John Smyth (10)	116
Christopher Logan (11)	117
Joseph McAllister (11)	117
Ciaran McCamphill (10)	117
Shannon Mullan (11)	118
Nicky McKeague (11)	118
James McFall (9)	118
Kieran Hughes (10)	119
Joseph Dowds (9)	119
Christy Drain (10)	119
Rebecca Lewis (9)	120
Adara McKendry (11)	120
Caitriona Boyle (11)	120
Sorcha Doherty (9)	121
Niamh McAuley (10)	121
James Kearns (9)	121
Sean Hurl (10)	121
Stephanie McKendry (10)	122
Keiran O'Loan (11)	122
Joanne Traynor (10)	122

Lauren Elliott (10)   123
Patrick Martin (11)   123
Paul Cochrane (10)   123
John O'Neill (9)   124
James McGowan (10)   124
Gemma Weir (10)   124
Caoimhe McCullagh (10)   125

St Joseph's Primary School, Crumlin
Amy McCorry (10)   125
Anne McAllister (9)   126
Kevin McCabe (10)   126
Kerry Woulfe (10)   127
Lauren Dwyer (9)   127
Nicole Donaghy (9)   127
Lucy Smart (10)   128
Tom Barnes (10)   128
Connor McCreanor (10)   129
Aoife McKavanagh (9)   129
Nadine McGarry (10)   130
Jarlath Mulhern (10)   130

St Mary's Primary School, Greenlough
Kate Lagan (8)   131
Paul Carey (9)   131
Jonathan McAteer (8)   132
Aidan McErlean (8)   132
Aimee Cassidy (9)   133
Roisin McCloskey (9)   133
Orla McErlean (7)   134
Niall Loughlin (9)   134
Michael Og Lagan (10)   135
Christopher McPeake (9)   135
Catherine Morren (9)   136
Emma Mooney (8)   136
Ryan McGoldrick (9)   137
Aimee Bedell (9)   137
Elish Madden (8)   138
Caolan Diamond (8)   138
Fionn Hamill (8)   139
Sarah McCann (8)   139

Claire McErlain (8)	140
Aine McErlean (8)	140
Michaela Lynn (7)	141
Caoimhe McNally (8)	141
Pauline Madden (10)	142
Shannon Rafferty (9)	142
Clare Doherty (10)	143
James Duffin (10)	143
Emma McErlain (9)	144
Gráinne Maguire (9)	144
Robert Kelly (10)	145
Colleen McErlean (10)	145
Shauna Quinn (10)	146
Seanin Marron (9)	146
Liza Marie Duffin (8)	147

St Patrick's & St Brigid's School, Ballycastle

Orlagh McAfee (8)	147
Ronan Blaney (8)	147
Mairead McHenry (9)	148
Jenny McHenry (8)	148
Hugh Neill (9)	149
Shane Devlin (8)	149
Bronagh McCaughan (8)	150
Shannon Mullan (7)	150
Ciarrai Guihan (8)	151
Alvin Baby (8)	151
Lisa Warn (7)	151
Darren McGuigan (8)	152
Jimmy McKiernan (8)	152
Elora-danan Kinney (8)	153
Sinéad Brown (8)	153
Catherine Curran (8)	153
Conor Spence (8)	154
Sean Maxwell (8)	154
Enya Kate De Wolf (8)	154
Cathal Connor (8)	155
Aoife Walsh (8)	155
Ronan McAfee (8)	155
Emma Smylie (8)	156
Riona McCambridge (7)	156

Daniel Morgan (8)	156
Fionnula Mooney (8)	157
Neill Ronald Duncan (9)	157
Caoimhe Hyland (9)	157
Erin McBride (8)	158
Abbie McNeill (9)	158
Alice Mee (9)	158
Rachel Woodhouse (8)	159
Laura McQuilkin (7)	159
Danielle McMichael (9)	159
Bronagh Clarke (8)	160
Megan Mooney (9)	160
Shannon Hegarty (9)	160
Hannah McMullan (7)	161
Tamara Mooney (7)	161
Ruairi Kinney (8)	162
Collum McKiernan (7)	162
Chloe Kelly (8)	163
Coleen Cahill (7)	163
Connor Norcott (7)	164
Rory Magee (8)	164
Ryan McFall (8)	165
Lindsay Horner (8)	165
Cliodhna Devlin (7)	166
Ronan McCarry (7)	166
Eoin McAuley (7)	167
Fiona Lagan (7)	167
Siobhan Donnelly (7)	168
Caolan McCaughan (7)	168
Kaelan Killough (8)	169
Una Staunton (8)	169
Caitilin Gormley (9)	170
Ruiari McKay (9)	170

The Diamond Primary School

Jamie Greer (8)	170
Rachael Carson (8)	171
Erin Herbison (7)	171
Matthew Kirk (8)	171
Ben Millar (8)	171
Niall Cavanagh (7)	172

The Poems

The Magic Box

(Based on 'Magic Box' by Kit Wright)

I will put in the box . . .
The sparkle of the stars,
A shimmering diamond of a crown,
The whitest snowflake of winter,
And the magic of my family.

I will put in the box . . .
The steam of an engine,
The clickety-clack of the coaches,
The poems of a book,
And the sky of a winter's evening.

I will put in the box . . .
The rattle of a snake,
The roar of a lion,
And the smudge of ink.

I will put in the box . . .
The crimson of a rose,
The wings of a butterfly,
And the feathers of a peacock.

I will put in the box . . .
The salt from the sea,
The black of a blackboard,
The gold of the sun,
And the light of the moon.

I will put in the box . . .
The copper of a penny,
The gush of a hurricane,
The rose petals sprinkled with dew.

For the covering I will put
Diamonds sprinkled with stardust,
I will keep it in a treasure chest forever.

Marcus McCullough (9)
Antrim Primary School

The Magic Box

(Based on 'Magic Box' by Kit Wright)

I will put in the box . . .
A sparkling golden egg,
Stardust that shines at night,
A deadly T-Rex with pure white fangs,
A crystal with sapphires all over,
The redness of the sunset
Also the gentle night's breeze,
The feeling of the soft silk.

Children laughing on Christmas Day,
The kindness of everybody around the world,
The magical sound of the snow falling,
The taste of ice cream on a sunny day.

A dragon's fang made from diamonds,
And a cat with a squeak and a mouse with a miaow,
A boxing kangaroo and a hopping boxer,
The joy of a baby taking its first step,
And last the golden moon inside a ruby-coated box.

Adam McClenaghan (10)
Antrim Primary School

The Magic Box

(Based on 'Magic Box' by Kit Wright)

I will put in the box . . .
A cobra that you can never catch,
The chatter of the rainforest,
The sight of the sun reflecting off the blue sea,
The coldness of a snowflake hitting your nose.

I will put in the box . . .
The sound of a baby's first laugh,
The taste of your hot dinner on a cold winter's night,
And the love of my family and friends.

I will put in the box . . .
The magic of St Nick,
The sound of ripping paper on Christmas day,
A kangaroo walking and a human hopping.

I will put in the box . . .
Memories of my classmates,
A diamond with a ruby-red coating,
And all the memories of the lives lost in the tsunami.

My box is made of diamonds with gold inside,
I will keep my box in a safe.

Jonathan Adams (9)
Antrim Primary School

My Magic Box

(Based on 'Magic Box' by Kit Wright)

I will put in the box . . .
The feeling of the morning,
The sun as round as an orange,
The whistle of an ocean in the
Middle of the night,
The sparkle of stardust in the palm
Of my hand,
The sound of Nelly going
Through my head.
I will put in the box . . .
A snowflake that never melts in the
Hot boiling sun,
The sound of kitten purring
In my ear,
The sound of my sister giggling away,
The feel of the sand in-between my toes,
The gleam of a diamond
On my finger.
My box would be made of
White gold,
With a diamond on top.

Saoirse Reed McCombe (10)
Antrim Primary School

The Magic Box

(Based on 'Magic Box' by Kit Wright)

I will put in the box . . .
The leathery smell of the inside of a
Brand new car,
The sound of a John Deere flying over the city,
The sound of a hyena laughing in the
African sunset.

I will put in the box . . .
The crash of a snowflake hitting the
Ground and the silence of a tree falling,
The biggest Christmas pudding with
Custard and cream,
The sound of a hurricane coming closer.

I will put in the box . . .
The feeling of golden sand slipping
Through my fingers,
A snowflake in the Sahara desert not melting,
The sound of one person skiing down the mountain.

My box is made of water and the lid is made
Of gold, sprinkled with diamonds,
It is kept in a secret place and if I told you,
I would have to kill you.

Adam Patterson (10)
Antrim Primary School

The Magic Box

(Based on 'Magic Box' by Kit Wright)

I will put in my box . . .
The magic and love of my family
The light of day and the dark of night
The crimson ruby-red and bright.

I will put in my box . . .
My history
The sound of the wind
Thoughts of life.

I will put in my box . . .
A promise to keep the world safe and clean
Take evil to an end
The way of peace instead of hate.

I will put in my box . . .
The life of a village
The waves of the sea
A book to share with your friends.

I will put in the box . . .
The smile of a baby
A part of my soul.

I will put in my box . . .
I will share my laugh
I will soar in the sky.

I will put in my box . . .
A man with more spells than my box
Beware of nothing
For it has been done.

I will put in my box . . .
The silence of the sky
I will put my box in the ocean
Like armour safe and strong.

Cameron Gibson (9)
Antrim Primary School

My Magic Box

(Based on 'Magic Box' my Kit Wright)

I will put in the box . . .
The breath of a fire-burning sun,
The sparkle of a gold moon,
The secrets that I'm never going to tell,
The juice of the driest lake,
The moo of a dog,
The silence of a scream,
The magic of the world,
And everything I've seen.

I will put in my box . . .
The most precious thing I have,
The memories of a lifetime,
The lightness of the dark,
The privilege of friends,
And the smelliest primrose ever,
The diamond-coated river,
The dullness of the rainbow.

I will put in my box . . .
My feelings sad and happy,
The harmony of joy,
The greatness of family,
The sound of the greatest orchestra,
The smells of a loving home,
The laughter of a lion.

The box will be made of
Chocolate covered walls with buttons over it,
The happiness of imagination,
And the softest words ever spoken,
Though you ask me where I keep it,
If I told you it wouldn't be a secret.

Nicole Kell (10)
Antrim Primary School

The Magic Box

(Based on 'Magic Box' by Kit Wright)

I will put in the box . . .
The delightful sound of a diamond bee
buzzing past a rose,
The sparkling snowflake at Christmas,
The first sound of my baby sister.

I will put in the box . . .
My true friends laughing at my jokes,
The 'oink' of a cow,
The 'moo' of a pig.

I will put in the box . . .
A horse riding on a cowboy,
The smile of my wonderful teacher,
My daddy's grave,
All the memories of the people out in Thailand,
Who lost their lives.

My box is made out of,
Diamonds, beautiful petals of a rose
And hot chocolate with marshmallows,
With a mermaid's purse in the middle.

I will keep my box,
Under my bed and I will let my granny's dog sleep
On it and she can keep the hot chocolate and
Marshmallows warm.

Chelsea McWilliams (10)
Antrim Primary School

The Magic Box

(Based on 'Magic Box' by Kit Wright)

I will put in the box . . .
The magic of Christmas and the mystery it holds,
The sound of rushing water on a crisp cool morning,
The power a ruler has over his kingdom.

I will put in the box . . .
A miracle that will never happen,
The ingredients of the nicest cake ever made,
A snowflake tumbling in the air before it reaches the ground.

I will put into the box . . .
A flower that will never die,
A feast with little food,
And a dinner with enough food to kill a man.

My box is made of steel and silver that will never break,
I will keep it in such a secret place, even I don't know where it is.

Andrew Burns (10)
Antrim Primary School

The Bully

Bullies don't wear badges,
They just look like you and me,
The things that make them different,
You can't always see.
The things that make them bullies,
Are the things they do and say,
Inside they must be very angry,
To make them act this way.

Olivia Pethick (11)
Ballymoney Model Primary School

Snow

What I hate about snow
Is the way people throw snowballs at you.

What I like about snow
Is the way the snow is white.

What I hate about snow
Is the way it gets you
In your face
And you get soaking wet!

What I like about snow
Is the way the snow glistens
In the sun.

What I hate about snow
Is the way the snow gets dirty
And it is very slippery
And when the snow blows in your face.

What I like about snow
Is the way it is soft
And very fun
And it is crisp and clean.

Natasha Lyttle (8)
Ballymoney Model Primary School

Bullying It Must Be Stopped!

There are these two boys in my class,
They throw stones and mud with grass,
They pick on a lot of people, but mostly me,
I can't take it anymore, I just want to be free,
I tried ignoring them, but that didn't work,
I tried telling the teacher, but she just laughed with a smirk,
I told my mum and she told the headmaster,
Then he talked to the bullies and it ended in disaster . . .
For them.

Andrew Mills (11)
Ballymoney Model Primary School

Snow

What I hate about snow
Is the way it is cold and slippery.

What I like about snow
Is building a snowman.

What I hate about snow
is when it turns into slush
And when it melts.

What I like about snow
Is when it covers the trees
And the way it is soft.

What I hate about snow
Is the way it gets in your face
And gets you soaking wet!

What I like about snow
Is the way it glistens in the sun
And the way it crunches
When you walk on it.

Leisha Woods (8)
Ballymoney Model Primary School

The Bully

When I enter the playground, I look around,
To see if the bully is anywhere to be found.

All hopes are lost, when I see him by the wall,
I try to run away, but he trips me up and I fall.

My knees are sore, my elbow too,
He's hurt me today - oh what can I do?

I hoped and prayed he would not be there,
But then I saw that terrible *glare*!

Something has to be done about that bully today,
To make our playground a safer place to play!

Laura Witherow (11)
Ballymoney Model Primary School

Snow

What I hate about snow
Is when the snow goes all slushy.

What I like about snow
Is I can make a snowman.

What I hate about snow
Is when people throw snowballs at me
And they hit me in the face!

What I like about snow
Is when the cars leave tracks
And I like the snow when it goes all gungy.

What I hate about snow
Is when I fall on the ice
And hurt my arm
And my leg.

Donovan Holmes (8)
Ballymoney Model Primary School

Bullying

I was a *bully* as bold as could be,
Who picked on a boy whose name was Lee,
He was very small and rather chubby,
That is why I called him Tubby.
Then one day my teacher challenged me,
About the horrible way I treated Lee.

Now I've changed, I'm a different guy,
So here I'll tell you the reason why,
Short or tall, fat or thin,
We are really all the same within,
And what I've discovered about my new friend Lee,
He likes football and PlayStation the same as me.

Gemma Glendinning (11)
Ballymoney Model Primary School

Snow

What I hate about snow
Is when people throw snowballs at me.

What I like about snow,
Is building snowmen.

What I hate about snow
Is when I slip,
And fall and
Hurt myself.

What I like about snow,
Is that it looks nice in
Your garden.

What I hate about snow
Is when the wind blows the snow
Goes in your face.

What I like about snow
Is that it's nice and Christmassy.

Elle Moore (8)
Ballymoney Model Primary School

Snow

What I hate about snow
Is the way people throw snowballs at me.

What I like about snow
Is you can make snowmen.

What I hate about snow
Is it's freezing cold
And when the sun comes out
The snow turns to slush.

What I like about snow
Is it's crisp and clean with fun around the corner
And when the snow flutters down and covers the ground.

Naomi McGregor (8)
Ballymoney Model Primary School

Snow

What I hate about snow
Is it makes your feet freezing.

What I like about snow
Is sledging down big hills.

What I hate about snow
Is when it turns to slush
It is all gooey and gungy
And you could get hit by a slushball.

What I like about snow
Is you can have massive snowball fights
If you get all your friends.

What I hate about snow
Is if you walk under a tree
A bit of snow could fall on you.

What I like about snow
Is that everybody
Gets to have fun in it.

Claire Crawford (8)
Ballymoney Model Primary School

The Bully

He stands for me at the gate,
For his victims he loves to wait,
He punches, he kicks and he calls me names,
He's a fun wrecker, he ruins my games,
To be kind and nice he really hates,
And that's the reason he's got no mates,
A bully is mean, a bully is bad,
A bully is secretly lonely and sad.

Andrew Hanna (11)
Ballymoney Model Primary School

Snow

What I hate about snow
Is the way it goes away.

What I like about snow
Is you get to throw snowballs.

What I hate about snow,
Is the way it gets in your face,
When people throw snowballs at you.

What I like about snow
Is it is so soft
And white
And crisp and clean.

What I hate about snow
It goes all gungy and slushy
And freezing.

What I like about snow
Is you get to make a snowman
And make footprints
And play outside.

Connor McIntyre (8)
Ballymoney Model Primary School

The Bully

Bullies are a pain in the brain
They get pleasure in causing other people pain,
I agree with the rest of the school,
If you are a bully you must be a fool,
So if you are a bully, please think twice,
Don't be cruel, it's better to be nice.

Jade Watton (10)
Ballymoney Model Primary School

Snow

What I hate about snow,
Is falling and we get wet.

What I like about snow,
Is building a snowman.

What I hate about snow,
Is the way it gets
In your face
And you get soaked.

What I like about snow,
Is making snowballs,
With my friends
And my dad.

Naomi Murdock (8)
Ballymoney Model Primary School

A Bully

A bully is a person,
Who *thinks* he's big and strong,
But when he finally meets his match,
He finds he's very wrong.

He picked on someone smaller,
And made his life so bad,
But now the bully has no friends,
This makes *him* rather sad.

Rachel McElfatrick (11)
Ballymoney Model Primary School

The Bully

I come to school, he's at the gate,
Oh no, I am going to be late.

Don't ask me, I can't see
Why the bully bullies me.

When I am out playing games
He calls me names.

Don't ask me I can't see
Why the bully bullies me.

He follows me home, I'm all alone,
He pushes me, I hurt my knee.

Don't ask me I can't see
Why the bully bullies me.

I tell the teacher the next day,
He's not allowed out to play,
He tells me why, he starts to cry,
Now I can see
Why the bully bullies me!

Mark Crooks (11)
Ballymoney Model Primary School

Holidays

What I like about going on holidays,
Is when you get a tan in the sun,
What I hate about going on holidays,
Is the long plane journey,
What I like about going on holiday,
Is going to the Water Park,
What I hate about going on holiday
Is when you go on the path and
It is hot on the ground.

Chloe Ballantine (7)
Ballymoney Model Primary School

Cars!

As slow as a turtle,
Cars as fast as a bullet,
Darting into the distance.

Cars as noisy as a tractor,
And as silent as a robin.

Bumper like a buffalo,
Spoiler like thunder,
And doors like a puff of wind.

Joseph Cross (9)
Broughshane Primary School

Spring

As yellow as the shiny sun,
Children are all around,
Running, skipping and jumping,
Happy as could be,
Adults are sleeping while children play,
Birds are soaring through brilliant blue sky.

Justin Jolly (9)
Broughshane Primary School

Spring

Spring is a wonderful season,
Baby lambs prancing in the cool, cool breeze,
Days are extended,
Nights get shorter,
Flowers are blooming,
People happy and cheerful,
Oh spring is a wonderful season!

Hayley Sloan (8)
Broughshane Primary School

My Puppies

M ilk is loved by my puppies,
Y elping, helping brothers and sisters.

P anting through night and day,
   working their heart all day.
U nwanted puppies all through the country,
P ay for puppies, ours are free, you'll not have to pay a fee!
P eople buying puppies,
 I ntergrated heating lamp heating the cute little barrels,
E verybody loves them night and day,
S oft little noses squeezing in your hands.

Philip McCullough (10)
Broughshane Primary School

Winter

In winter we have so much fun,
Running about and seeing the sun,
Building big fat snowmen,
Eating a big fat hen.

Having so much fun,
And having a good bun,
Eat up all your food,
And enjoy your favourite pud!

Ross Clyde (10)
Broughshane Primary School

Spring

Lambs are playing,
Birds are singing,
Buds opening every day,
Rabbits hopping,
Cows are laying down,
Daffodils bathing in the sun.

Jason Nicoletti (9)
Broughshane Primary School

What Summer Means To Me

Summer is a lovely time,
When flowers come up,
And sun comes down,
Water always cools us down,
When we're hot and sweaty in the town.

I like to sing and skip in summer,
And I always like to play with others,
Spring, autumn and winter are not the same,
For when it's summer there is nothing to complain.

When it's summer it's as hot as toast,
Not like winter when it's fun, but cold,
Every day of the year I play,
But summer is my favourite time,
When you can hop around at any time.

Katie Carrington (9)
Broughshane Primary School

My Best Friends

My best friends,
Adele, Jane and Eva too,
Adele is giddy,
Jane is kiddy,
And Eva's very smart,
We all like art,
Always doing our part,
They're my friends,
They're lots of fun,
And that's the end of my poem,
I hope it gets shown,
And now we will all go,
To play in the sun!

Ruth Foster (8)
Broughshane Primary School

Kel

Kel likes the Cha Cha Slide,
Kel is always happy,
Kel's favourite drink is orange soda,
Kel is always at home,
Kel's favourite colour is blue,
Kel doesn't like dresses,
Kel's happy with his clothes,
Kel thinks his home is cool!

Leea Mark (7)
Broughshane Primary School

My Mum

You're like the pinkest sunset,
You're like the swing in the people's park,
You're like my fluffy sweater,
You're a yummy hot chocolate on a long winter's day,
You're a spicy Chinese,
You make me dance to pop music,
I love you.

Megan Palmer (8)
Broughshane Primary School

Bethany

You're like the colour pink,
Your eyes shine like the Coke in a cup,
You like McDonald's and so do I,
You are my best friend,
You make me feel warm like a scarf,
You are good at singing,
You make me feel at home,
You make me feel happy.

Lauren Chambers (8)
Broughshane Primary School

Steven G

You're like the clearest sky,
You're like a cold, cold drink of Coca-Cola that makes
me cold in the summer.
You're like a Rangers' player in the Rangers' kit,
You're like a Chinese that makes me warm,
You're like a kangaroo jumping,
You make me feel like I'm in Spain,
You're like a pop dance,
You're my best friend.

Aaran Weir (8)
Broughshane Primary School

What Winter Means To Me

W inter is a dusky and dull time,
 I cy roads are lubricious and slippery,
N ot the best time of year that's for sure,
T rees are bare as bare as can be,
E arly wings of happiness hit the sky,
R eindeers are at the ready.

Adam Heron (10)
Broughshane Primary School

Lois

You're like the pinkest sunset in the world,
When I see you I hear Girls Aloud,
You make me taste chips and chicken,
You're like orange juice from a cup,
You look like the nicest poncho,
You feel like home,
You make me happy,
Lois you're my best friend ever.

Bethany Armstrong (7)
Broughshane Primary School

Shannon

You're like my most favourite purple toy on my whole shelf,
You lightened up my day like when I listen to Swan Lake,
You feel like some tasty steak pie in my hungry tum,
When you cheer me up in warmth, it's like a hot cup of tea,
You make me feel like I'm floating in the air in a wedding dress,
You make me feel like I am in a golden field singing to nature,
When you smile you sometimes make me shy,
Shannon you're the best friend a girl could have.

Amy McWhirter (8)
Broughshane Primary School

Bethany

You're like a pink, blue and purple sunset,
You're like a singer out of Girls Aloud,
You're like my high heels,
You make me feel happy when I am sad,
You are like the warmth of my home,
You are like cool orange juice,
You are like hot chips and chicken.

Catherine McBurney (8)
Broughshane Primary School

James

You're like a ripe purple plum,
You are like rock playing,
You are like Five Alive running down my throat,
You are like jeans and my favourite top,
You make me feel like I'm at home,
You're like my favourite Chinese,
You make me laugh so much it hurts.
You are my best friend.

Philip Weir (8)
Broughshane Primary School

David

You can run at fast as a red fire engine,
You can dance to rock music,
I could squeeze you like a burger,
You are my best friend,
You are like a cold drink of cola when I am hot,
You love your football kit,
You love coming to my house,
You make me happy.

Christopher Burrows (8)
Broughshane Primary School

Christopher

You are like the blue of the school jumper,
You are like Elvis singing on stage,
You make me feel like a whole sausage out
Of a Chinese in my belly,
Christopher is my best friend,
You swim down my throat like apple juice,
You fit like a football kit in the summer,
You are like a games shop,
You are like an angry bull.

David Craig (7)
Broughshane Primary School

Philip

You're like the darkest red of a football shirt,
You're like rock music at the disco,
You're like yummy pizza and chips,
You're like hot chocolate with marshmallows,
You're like a new jacket,
You make me laugh until it hurts,
You are like a jet going to Spain,
You are my best friend.

Robbie Erwin (7)
Broughshane Primary School

Pets

I have a dog not a hog,
He's black and white, and a lovely sight.

I have a cat not a bat,
She's grey and white and loves the light.

I have a hamster not a banister,
She's pale and white and has a good bite.

So you've come to the end of my poem,
I hope you've had good fun,
The only thing I hope it's done is
Bring out the burning sun.

Joseph Murray (9)
Broughshane Primary School

Philip

You make me feel like I have drumming in my head,
You are like a drink of Five Alive,
Your clothes are so sporty, you look like a footballer,
You invite me over to your house,
You make me laugh till it hurts,
You are like burger and chips,
You are my best friend.

James Robinson (8)
Broughshane Primary School

Rodney

You're like my Manchester United football kit,
You're like chips with red sauce,
You're cosy like my home,
You're like the blue sky,
You're like cold milk,
You make me dance like pop music,
You make me happy.

Richard Sloan (7)
Broughshane Primary School

Rosslyn

You're like a pink flower,
You're like my new dress,
You're like chips and sausage,
You're like pop music,
You make me happy,
You're like milk,
You make me feel at home,
Rosslyn you're my best friend.

Lauren Robinson (7)
Broughshane Primary School

Gary

You're like the cleanest pink flower,
You're like a cold cup of milk on a summer's night,
You make me dance when I listen to Pop Party,
You make me feel cosy like my pink scarf,
You make me happy when I look at you,
When I go to Bally Keel I think of you every day,
You're like a cheeseburger,
You are my best friend.

Michaela Mark (8)
Broughshane Primary School

Rebecca

You are like a number 1 in the charts,
You are like the blue sea,
You are like fizzy cola,
You are like chips and sauce,
You make me comfortable like black trousers.

Rosslyn McDowell (8)
Broughshane Primary School

Amy

You're like my soft fluffy poncho,
You're like the light blue sky,
You're always with me at the park,
You're like a hot cup of chocolate,
You're a big plate of chips,
You sound like Girls Aloud,
You always make me happy,
Amy, you are my best friend.

Shannon Beckett (7)
Broughshane Primary School

Gary

You are loud like pop music,
You are like sausages,
You make me feel happy,
You are like nice coke,
You are warm like my sweater,
You make me feel at home,
You're like my blue Ford 76B,
You are my friend.

Peter Millar (8)
Broughshane Primary School

Richard

You're like a shiny black sports car,
You're like a brand new pop tune,
You're like a football,
You're like a big pizza with tomato sauce,
You're like my silver and black football boots,
You're like the feeling I get when Coke fizzes up my nose,
You're like my home.

Rodney Magee (7)
Broughshane Primary School

Adam

Your eyes are like crystal pools of mud,
You make me dance under the disco lights,
You're like spicy chilli with satay sauce,
Adam you're my best friend,
You're like a warm cup of hot chocolate,
You're like my warm coat,
I like it when I see you at school,
You make me laugh until it hurts.

Kristian Douglas (7)
Broughshane Primary School

Mum

You're like the voice of rock on radio,
You make me the tastiest toast I ever tasted,
You're like the red skies of the night,
You look like a Coca-Cola bottle,
You make me laugh so much it hurts,
You look like a Man Utd football kit,
When I was at Newcastle I saw you on the rides.

Marc McDowell (7)
Broughshane Primary School

Dad

You're like the clearest red sunset,
You're like a cold sup of Sprite on a summer's night,
You're a slimy plate of spaghetti,
You make me crazy until it hurts,
You make me cosy when I'm in bed,
You make me dance when I listen to Britney Spears,
I like seeing you back from work in Madrid
Dad, you're my best mate.

Adam Ruck (8)
Broughshane Primary School

Spring Is Coming

Spring is coming,
Winter is leaving,
Flowers are popping out,
More sun than rain,
Kids playing footy,
No more snowdrops for a year,
Time to plant flowers,
Rugby games on big fields,
Winter ice and snow is forgotten,
Heatwaves coming soon.

Alexander Cole (9)
Broughshane Primary School

House Rules

You bring it out, you put it in
You make a mess, you clean it up!
If you dirty it, you clean it!
If you break it, you mend it!
If you do it, you flush it!
If you open it, you close it!
If you follow these rules, you're in!

Lewis Ferguson (8)
Broughshane Primary School

Teacher

Today I am sitting in class
I discover that I am staring
Very hard at my teacher
In a special way
I am able to put her to sleep
Hooray! No lessons today.

Alan Adams (8)
Broughshane Primary School

A Netball Match Was Coming Soon

A netball match was coming soon,
We had to practise, practise,
A netball match was coming soon,
We were getting over excited.

A netball match that we would win,
Play low, stay low,
A match that we could win,
Dodge the people we are playing,
Like a rubbish bin.

At the match, we could score,
Lots of goals, down to the core,
At the match, we could score,
Ten or more goals, right out the door.

Me and my team,
Could beat them easy,
Me and my team.
Should practise till we're queasy.

A netball match that we won,
A netball match, oh it was fun,
We beat them through, the match, we won!

Jane Montgomery (9)
Broughshane Primary School

School Is Boring!

School is boring,
But it helps you learn,
Try and make it interesting,
Do a good turn.

If you are still bored,
You can just read,
But if you don't have a book,
You're definitely in need!

Courtney Montgomery (9)
Broughshane Primary School

Sport

Football, cricket, tennis too,
How I would love to play it,
At school and on TV,
Every hour of the night.

Everybody plays it,
Everyone's the best,
I would love to be too,
Cousins, brothers all play it,
All except me.

Everyone around,
Asks me to play,
But when I do we always lose,
I always say I'm no good,
They never listen to me,
I wish they would for once,
Then I wouldn't be embarrassed.

I always want to learn,
How to play the games,
When I go home all I want
Is a nice cooked turkey.

Sport, sport, sport all the same,
Just for once can we win for once in my life!

Samuel McCartney (8)
Broughshane Primary School

Spring

S ummer is on its way,
P leasant flowers about to grow,
R olling our Easter eggs down Slemish Mountain,
I love spring - my favourite season,
N ewborn lambs playing in the fields,
G oing to the travel agent's to book our holidays.

Gemma McAlonan (9)
Broughshane Primary School

My Grandparents

My granny played for Scotland,
She nearly scored a goal,
She did the splits,
And had some nits,
And Granny hit a pole.

My grandad played for France,
And he really loved to dance,
He felt so giddy,
That he looked rather silly,
When he drove his little Mini.

My grandparents!
My grandparents!
Are always very stupid,
They love their reindeer Cupid,
So I guess you understand,
They're utterly stupid!

Jordan Miller (9)
Broughshane Primary School

The Alien Invasion

When I was in my bed last night,
Aliens came through my door,
One looked tall,
The other small,
Where was their spaceship?
That was what I wondered.
But there's definitely aliens out there,
Raiding houses all around town,
In and out they go,
Watch out people of the world.
Outer space invades.

Adele Getty (9)
Broughshane Primary School

Winter

Dull, dark days
Long, black nights
Grey, cloudy skies
Christmas lights.

Windowpanes glisten
Pavements snowy and deep
Icicles hang from rooftops
Shiny stars peep.

Branches are bare
Colour has gone
Birds fly south
Frost in the morn.

Hats, scarves, gloves and boots
Our cheeks are glowing red
The snowman stands in the cold
We are warm in bed.

These things mean winter
People are sad
But soon spring is coming
Then we will be glad.

Victoria Gault (8)
Broughshane Primary School

The First Of September

New shoes,
Nice ebony colour,
New bags,
With books piling in,
New pencils,
With leads as sharp as pins,
New classmates,
What a fun time to make friends!

Philip Stevenson (9)
Broughshane Primary School

My Pet Pony

My pony is exciting and fun,
He can really, really run,
As far as the green hill,
To meet up with his friend Bill.

I call him Bob,
Because he has a cosy job,
As I bring him hay,
I can hear him neigh.

He lets me plait his tail,
If I tell him a short tale.
He can eat apples to a band parade,
But he doesn't like lemonade.

He bit my little brother,
A day like no other.
Al never came back to see him,
Because he thought Bob was a greedy bin.

Gayle Adams (10)
Broughshane Primary School

My Puppy

Soft, cute and messy,
Brown, black and white,
Sometimes he can be dangerous,
Sometimes he can be bright.

My puppy is silly,
My puppy is cool,
What will he do next?
Go to the swimming pool!

Altogether my puppy is mine,
Mine to keep
If I really can't find him
He's playing hide-and-seek.

Jaymee O'Hara (8)
Broughshane Primary School

Find Me A . . .

Down by the beach on a stormy day,
Find me a seal, in a salty spray.
Lurking in the swamp where nobody goes,
Find me a crocodile with a long, pointy nose.
Over the mountains soaring high,
Find me an eagle with sharp, beady eyes.

Out on the plain lazing around,
Find me a male lion, with a deafening sound.
Tucked under a leaf while the day goes by,
Find me a frog that's very shy.
Out in the desert with a rock for a shield,
Find me a snake rattling its tail.
Under a bush, cold with the chill,
Find me a fawn, lying quite still.

Down by the waterhole, taking a drink,
Find me an alert animal that looks like a lynx.
Deep in the woods running about
Find me a naughty fox that needs a good clout.

Zara Thompson (10)
Broughshane Primary School

My Pets

My guinea pig
It looks like it wears a wig,
My dog is so very caring,
It is also very daring,
My cat drinks out of the tap,
When it's tired, it lives on your lap,
My horse is mostly full of hay,
When he gets out in the morning, he loves to play,
At night my cat gets put into the shed,
And then I go to bed.

Jack Gourley (9)
Broughshane Primary School

The Match On Springfield Street

The match was played on Springfield Street,
By boys who were naughty, nice and neat.
Stupid, smart, it did not matter,
Some were thin and some were fatter.

Some were nine and some were ten,
Some were as big as fully-grown men.
If you were there, you'd kick the ball,
And probably have the occasional fall.

It didn't matter if it was rain or snow,
Some of the boys were sure to go.
There was a match every day,
From December right through to May.

To this game there were no rules,
Anyone could play, from dogs to bulls.
The game lasted from dawn to dusk,
Even the bikes at the side had started to rust.

After the game they went home to bed,
Dreaming of playing at Wembley instead.
In the morning they'd feed the hamster in its pen,
Then they'd be off to do it again.

Philip Cunningham (10)
Broughshane Primary School

Winter

W oolly gloves on our hands keeping them nice and warm.
 I nside, the fire is lit to keep me snug and warm.
N ight comes, night goes, I'm snug in my bed, Jack Frost
    comes creeping out of the shed.
T rees go bare, as white as a stallion.
E ating turkey at the table.
R obin redbreast comes out to seek his prey at night, he has to eat.

Hollie Neeson (9)
Broughshane Primary School

My Pet

I have a dog called Meg
She is very big and shaggy
And whenever I take her for a walk
She jumps in the river
And starts to splash.
Meg eats and eats
Until she is so fat she can hardly walk.

She likes to jump and play with me
And chases butterflies and bees
I love to take her out for walks
Because I love her to bits.
She's got a ball that she loves to play with
And she rolls it about with her nose.
I love my dog so much
Even though she is a bit of trouble.

Chloe McGall (10)
Broughshane Primary School

My Pets

I have a dog called Tancho,
I have a cat called Snowey,
Every time they see me they want me to play with them,
I love them all,
And they love me.

The dog and cat, they love each other,
Having fun each day,
I am glad they like living with me,
Running around,
Making a mess for me to clear up!
But I still love them.

Caroline Fleck (9)
Broughshane Primary School

Tourism

So many places to see
So many places you want to be
From Eiffel Tower to the Grand Canyon
I've lost count of tourist sights
Too many countries to see them all
The world's a great massive ball
Seven continents, absolutely amazing!

Thousands of cities
Full of life
From New York to Moscow
Billions of towns and villages
I would like to explore the world
But no one can visit every attraction.

A city, a little dot on the globe
But so big when you're there
Earth must be trillions of square miles
Then some people wreck the world
That is stupid, do you agree?

Adam McDowell (11)
Broughshane Primary School

The Great Snowman

Great big snowmen
Smiling in the gardens,
Fat and thin, but all akin.
Orange carrot noses,
Black, dirty buttons.

Pink, purple, red and blue
Woolly hats snowmen love to wear
Brown, little, thin arms,
    I love snow
    I love snowmen!

Sarah Kennedy (10)
Broughshane Primary School

Pets All Around Us!

Cats and dogs are all around us
Guinea pigs as well
Having fun together
Every single day.
In my garden,
In my lane,
In my house as well.
Skipping, jumping, running round
Up the stairs and down.
Making a mess for me to clean
What clumsy pets they are
But I still love them
Every bit and more.

Amy Hunter (9)
Broughshane Primary School

Winter Wonderland

Sparkling snowflakes falling down
A white, crispy, snowy blanket lying on the ground
Building snowmen, throwing snowballs
Down the chimney Santa crawls.

Leaving presents for you and me
Jumping out of bed on Christmas Day to see what he has left
beneath the tree.
Shouting and cheering, opening your toys with happy joys.

Eating your Christmas dinner,
It doesn't make you get thinner
Lying in the house, nice and cosy
Making your cheeks go rosy.
I wonder if it's still *winter wonderland!*

Joanne Stirling (9)
Broughshane Primary School

Scrooge

I am Scrooge, all mean and nasty,
All day long I count my money.
And I am rich and very greedy,
I never share with anyone.
Never give to charity or to the poor,
I am Scrooge and no one else.
But now come three ghosts,
To haunt me and teach me a lesson.
First it's Past,
Second, it's Present,
And finally the third, the worst of them all
It is Future,
He shows me my grave and it's morbid and cold.
What a nightmare!
Now it is morning, all sunny and bright,
I'm a changed man, kind and thoughtful.
Thank you spirits.

David Murray   (11)
Broughshane Primary School

My Dog Ally

My dog Ally has floppy ears,
It's almost as though his teeth are spears.
He loves it when I give his belly a scratch,
When I throw his ball he goes after it in a dash.

Sometimes Ally is a mass,
But sometimes he rolls about on the grass.
Of course Ally is a boy,
And loves to play with his toy.

My dog Ally is really fast,
I can hardly see him when he flies past.
When he's in the car, it's such a cram,
We're on our way for a walk to the dam.
That's my dog Ally!

Calvin Kernohan   (10)
Broughshane Primary School

Wintertime

Wintertime is really fun,
All the snow, frost and ice comes.
Children playing in the snow,
Snow is here, hip hip hooray.

Christmastime is nearly here,
Santa Claus is getting ready,
For his big, long trip,
Snow is here, hip hip hooray.

Christmas Eve is today,
I can't wait until tomorrow,
To get to open all my presents,
Snow is here, hip hip hooray.

Now Christmas is finally here,
I rush down the stairs to open my presents.
Santa has left me all I asked for,
Christmas is here, hip hip hooray.

New Year's Day is here,
People celebrating 2006.
Some people make new year's resolutions,
2006 is here, hip hip hooray.

Andrew Millar (11)
Broughshane Primary School

Spring

S pring is here flowers pop up,
P eople come and spread seeds,
R ain comes in the springtime,
  I n spring lambs are born in a farmer's barn,
N obody hates spring because of the flowers,
G reat animals are born in spring.

Jak Palmer (10)
Broughshane Primary School

My Little Brother

My brother's name is Kristian
We call him Kris sometimes
And even though he's seven years old
He's naughty all the time.

He hides my shoes and books
He loses all my things
Kris always embarrasses me
The most he embarrasses me
Is when he starts to sing.

Kris always fights with me
And my mum blames me
I always get grounded up in my room
While he laughs, *ha, ha, ha!*

Mum called for tea one day
And we rushed to the table
After I had finished I ran to my room
But even though he follows me
I love him all the same.

Shannon Douglas (10)
Broughshane Primary School

I Like . . .

I like going swimming with my school.
I like playing pool with my dad.
I like playing darts with my friends.
I like playing cricket with my mates.
I like cycling with my cousins.
I like playing bowls with my grandad.
But best of all I like playing football with my football team.

Philip Scroggie (11)
Broughshane Primary School

My Playful Puppy

'Rex! Leave my slippers!
Please don't chew my toe.
Rex! Leave my sock,
Or my mum says you'll have to go.'

I sent him to puppy training
You've guessed! - It didn't work.
My dad even tried to train him
But that stopped when he scored his 'Merc'!

He messes on the carpet
And scores the wooden floor
He barks when our friendly postman . . .
Tries to put letters through the door!

My friends really do not like him
He chases their football like 'Becks',
He scares our neighbour's pussy,
But I love my puppy . . . *Rex!*

Samuel McNabney (11)
Broughshane Primary School

Predators

Predators hiding in amongst the grass
And in amongst the trees,
Jumping out at any time,
Bringing prey down to knees.

Predators, chasing and catching,
Prey being chased and caught,
Predators just want to survive,
From their mums and dads they have been taught.

Predators have long, sharp teeth,
And when hunting will never make a sound,
So don't make one angry,
Or it'll jump on you and bring you to the ground.

Christopher Smyth (11)
Broughshane Primary School

Steven Gerrard

Steven packs up and puts his clothes in his cases,
And when he gets to Anfield he strikes it with his laces.
Stevie has a sweet right foot,
And every match he wears a different boot.

Gerrard has all the skills,
And he does not take any pills.
He has got the predator pulse,
But people think they are false.

Gerrard has fair hair and is aged 24,
And when he scores at Anfield everyone lets out a roar!
When Gerrard gets the ball no one can catch him,
All they can do is let him score.

Lee McGavock (11)
Broughshane Primary School

Football

Football is my favourite sport
I like it very much
Kicking the ball into the net
Passing the ball to all my mates
Keeping it from the rest.

Tackling, throwing, kicking, scoring
Running fast to get the ball
Amidst the clapping, shouting, roaring
The ball it goes from side to side
All adds up to an exciting match.

Jolon Cupples (10)
Broughshane Primary School

Why Is Billy Sad?

Why is Billy sad?
Is he unaccompanied?
Has he been bad?
Or has he been hurt?

Is Billy sad because he's alone
Or is he in debt?
Is his mum still on the phone
Or has he messed up today?

Why is Billy sad?
Has his dog run away?
Has his sister gone bad?
No, no, his family has shut him out!

Nathan Houston (11)
Broughshane Primary School

The World's Greatest Pup!

My pup Tuppence, she can be a bit of a pain,
When I'm watching TV she drives me insane,
Oh Tuppence, what's that smell?
Now I'll have to go and tell.

All she does is sleep all day,
When she wakes up she goes out to play,
Her favourite is extras from our dinner,
If we have an eating race, she's always the winner.

Tuppence and her mum have such a good time,
Now I'm finishing off the rhyme,
I hope they're still having a good time.

Catherine McCartney (10)
Broughshane Primary School

Mist Fairy

She flies through the air with a smoky trail,
Blocking out the past.
Looking at her brother's sparkling frost,
Wishing she was him.

She envies his sparkling beauty
Glittering on the road.
Her dull, dark greyness lingers in alleyways,
How she wishes she was him.

But then one frosty night she thought
Why do I want to be him, his heart is icy and cold.
I'm glad I'm me.
I'm free to weave through deserted streets,
Leaving trails of long forgotten dreams.
A gossamer blanket of comfort.

Jenni McCandless (11)
Broughshane Primary School

Through The Mirror

I woke, I was startled
What was it?
Not my alarm
Then I heard it again
I thought I was dreaming
But I got up anyway
It seemed to be coming from my mirror
When I looked in the mirror
I wasn't in my silk pjs
I saw the dress in the mirror again
When I lifted my hands they were covered in mud
It was the dress
I touched the mirror and my hands went through!
I was *terrified!*

Alice McCaughey (10)
Broughshane Primary School

Is There An Answer?

Why don't we share food?
Why don't we share clothes?
Why don't we share money?
Only the Lord knows.

Why don't we stay friends?
Why aren't we positive?
Why don't we help each other?
After all He died for us to live.

Why is there fighting?
Why do we go to war?
I cannot understand.
What is it all for?

Why doesn't He stop this?
Why is the pain still here?
Why are we still quarrelling?
Is there an answer?

Stacey McGavock (11)
Broughshane Primary School

Animals

Animals big, animals small,
Animals spotty, animals jumpy,
Animals stripy, animals of the world.

Ones that can swim,
Ones with massive wings,
Ones with really long tails.

Cute, but sad, wide brown eyes,
Cute little kittens, what a surprise,
Cute little things are animals.

Animals of all kinds.

Nicola Galbraith (10)
Broughshane Primary School

Violet, The Star

I wish I could be famous,
I wish I could have power,
I wish I could be rich,
I wish I were a star.

Why can't I fly?
Why can't I have a friend?
Why won't anyone play with me?
I wish the world to end.

I wish someone could hear me,
Maybe watch me dance,
Or listen to me sing,
I might still have a chance.

I'll go out and find someone,
Someone who will listen to me,
Someone who will give me courage,
Someone to make my fears flee.

Nicole Bradley (10)
Broughshane Primary School

Martha The Giraffe

Birds, you better watch out when you fly,
You might hit Martha in the eye,
Martha can't help being so tall,
You might want to move quickly if you are small!

She lives in the jungle far, far away,
Where all the animals love to play,
She goes to the lake at half-past noon,
And will sit there till she sees the moon.

She has lovely big ears, which are brown and yellow,
And has a voice, which is soft and mellow,
Her short knobbed horns, all fluffy and clean,
She looks at herself in the mirror of the stream.

Abigail Martin (11)
Broughshane Primary School

Spring

Sping is here
With a cheer
Spring is here
Like every year
Spring, spring
What a thing!
It changes everything,
Old things become new
Because Santa has just been too.
A picture of God's creation is painted in your head
And who ate that apple so red?
Bright colours are used
Not much about spring is on the news
Daffodils come out
Lambs are here too.

Laura Millar (9)
Broughshane Primary School

Pharaoh

Pharaoh fights friends and foes,
While bakers knead fine doughs.
Pharaoh sits on his throne eating figs,
While slaves collect logs and twigs.

Pharaoh worships his fake gods,
While a slave starves and sobs.
Pharaoh's men build his tombs,
While Ra plans his doom.

Pharaoh waits for the Nile to flood,
While rival armies spill Egypt's blood.
Pharaoh's reign comes to an end,
Egypt will never mend.

Gary McKendry (11)
Broughshane Primary School

Our Dog Roxy

Roxy is playful and fun,
She is cute and graceful,
She is easy to love,
She likes to lick the wall
And chase the ball,
She's our house muppet
And everybody loves her.

Samantha Millar (9)
Broughshane Primary School

Beautiful Garden

Beyond the garden gate I walk,
down the steep and rugged hill;
I come to meet a weathered door, how awful it looks today.
I push against it, but it stands tall and firm,
then I begin to wonder what might be behind that door.
Maybe there are thousands of snapdragons,
or a maze with walls of ivy,
maybe there are trees everywhere you look,
with little bushes of lavender at their feet,
and the enchanting scent of climbing roses filling the air.
If only reality could be as wonderful as the imagination.

Katie Hamilton (9)
Carnaghts Primary School

My Puppy

I have a little puppy,
He is black and white,
He always licks my ears
Before bedtime every night.
I love him and he loves me
He's the cutest little dog
You will ever see.

Heather Steele (9)
Carnaghts Primary School

Sarah Elizabeth

S arah Wilson is my name,
A mazing good work is my aim.
R unning races is what I like to do.
A cting makes a good second too.
H elp, I've still got more to do.

E ating pizza and chips is what I like best.
L ove from my mum I put to the test.
I love to
Z zzzzzzz in my nest.
A nts and crawly things I detest.
B all games are what I like best.
E nergy I have in excess.
T ree huts which are a mess.
H elp, my mum says I must clean up the mess.

Sarah Wilson (10)
Carnaghts Primary School

Sea Life

Under the ocean far below,
the fish and mammals come and go.
There are fierce sharks that chase their prey,
and dolphins who just want to play.
The whales come up to breathe
and sprinkle water in the breeze.
In the warm seawater
there are tropical fish of every colour.
The octopus may not have charms
but it can squirt ink, and has eight long arms.
Conger eels hide in the rocks,
while their electric cousins give us shocks.
At night I wonder if they sleep
in a bedroom in the deep.

Lauren Todd (10)
Carnaghts Primary School

The Sea

Behold! I'm the ferocious sea,
I'm giant and grey,
I fight with my fists,
kick with my feet,
I clash my knuckles against the rocks,
I'm ready to come forward to wrestle and confront my foe.

Behold! Jealous I am
with the pretty sand,
all the youngsters caressing her golden hair,
and I want to declare a fight,
By slapping, scrabbing and strangling,
but she refuses because she's too gentle-natured.

Kathryn McFadden (10)
Carnaghts Primary School

Monty The Mouse

Monty was an inquisitive mouse,
He loved to explore,
One morning he set off. He went . . .
Through the scorching hot sand,
Along the wet, damp shore,
Under the holidaymakers' sunbeds,
On top of the beach café's platform,
Over the sea's frothy waves,
Behind the ice cream van,
Up to the beach shop where he bought a tiny toy boat,
Into the tiny toy boat and he sailed away.

Ruth Gracey (10)
Carnaghts Primary School

My Life As A Whiteboard Marker!

The door sprang open!
I'd been sitting in that box for ages,
Not a soul to speak to, not a thing to do,
Boy was it good to see the classroom light on again . . .
. . . And then she picked me up and took me over to the
big, special ledge,
At last, I've finally made it to where the teacher's pens stay,
I was now promoted, hooray!
But I've learnt that moments like this never last.

The nightmare began when the scallywags came in . . .
. . . Oh no . . . the urchins picked me up
And just scribbled with me . . .
They left my lid open,
The thing I hated most

Well, as sure as day is day,
I started to dry up,
I wish I was a fountain pen because it can be refilled,
I knew I would meet my maker, the great whiteboard marker!

Melissa O'Neill (11)
Carnaghts Primary School

The Cat!

I once saw a cat sit at the bottom of a tree
gazing at the beloved birds,
that were just about to flee.

Later I saw the same cat,
this time it was chasing a rat.
It was so tired, it had to take a nap.

Chloe McDonald (10)
Carnaghts Primary School

The Fire

Behold the fantastic reappears . . .

It was on a starry eve in autumn.
They lit the wood from a spark . . .
I was born.
I had a great big stretch,
I was ready to burn people in my flames,
My burning coat, and inject them with
my lung-filling poison.
And then I ventured towards the building,
but out of the corner of my eye, I saw it . . .
The big, red, six-legged monster
standing there ready to roar!

Shane McBurney (10)
Carnaghts Primary School

My Secret Companion

Any time of day or night,
He's always ready to wrestle or fight,
I get to jump around and shout,
Then along comes Mum and sends me out,
'You're messing things up!' I hear her scold,
But he started it, if the truth be told,
Later on I'll catch the cat,
Stretched out asleep like a furry mat,
Soon it's time for me to join Ted,
Fast asleep in my cosy little bed,
And there I lie, warmly cocooned,
As if on a tropical island, marooned.

Ross Hutchinson (10)
Carnaghts Primary School

The Cloud

Behold, I am mighty,
I am strong.
Who dares fight me will be drenched,
I spit rain
And sneeze snow,
When I downpour, the whole world
Will know.

I meet my enemy,
I face my foe,
I punch and kick,
But I won't stop,
I won't give up,
I'll raise a storm,
The wind punches me,
Slowly I lose strength,
I'll keep going,
I won't stop fighting,
I'll show him who's boss.

He shoots an arrow,
He punctures me,
My wound is dripping,
I've lost my battle,
I crash to the ground!

Sam Steele (11)
Carnaghts Primary School

Beautifully

Beautifully the horse raced through the meadow
Beautifully the horse jumped over the poles
Beautifully the horse grazed in the field
Beautifully the horse rolled in the sand
Beautifully the horse went into the meadow
And through the gushy river.

Neil Armstrong (10)
Carnaghts Primary School

Little Robin

Little robin I can see
Looking for berries for his tea.

Little robin I can see
Stealing twigs from a tree.

Little robin I can see
Flying as fast as a bee.

Little robin I can see
Working through reality.

Little robin needs a rest
Quickly sleeps with head on breast.

Little robin has woken up
Full of energy ready to erupt.

Little robin can see me
Off he flies to nearest tree.

Jordon Lynn (11)
Creavery Primary School

Red Squirrel

Escape, escape, stay alive today,
Death is formed as owl and grey.
His hardship never dies away.
His tail softer than silk.
His eyes twinkle like golden coins.
His wisdom more than an owl's
His speed faster than lightning.

Escape, escape, stay alive today,
Death is formed as owl and grey.
His hardship never dies away.
Dare not glance, dare not stop.
Danger lurks his way.
Owl is a tyrant in his heart.
Grey, a brother, hatred pulled apart.

Andrew Warwick (11)
Creavery Primary School

Beautiful Swan

Down the river to and fro,
Bobs a bird with a lot to show.
Admire it, look at it, gaze all you like,
Do not disturb though, or it will take flight.

White velvet feathers as bright as can be,
On the darkest, dullest ever a sea.
Piercing black eyes like a panther's coat,
Dancing around like a buoy afloat.

With its long slender neck, the swan reaches all,
Always so proud, with never a fall.
Its elegant jaw, that is made to deceive,
Can throw a sharp snap, like you'd never believe.
So now you can see the swan's great beauty,
Finished with an edge of fear.
It can glide through the sky or slide through the bay,
But beware of a bite on your rear!

Hannah Dennison (11)
Creavery Primary School

In The Playground . . .

P eople crying because they fall.
L oud voices make me jump when I walk past.
A nna, my sister, is watching the birds that sing so
   beautifully and quietly.
Y ells and screams come from every corner.
G roggan, I think, is the noisiest school.
R achael and her gang spying on people.
O ur friends giggle when we tell them a funny story.
U sually there's nobody who hasn't fallen by the end of the year.
N aomi pushed me over and made me cry.
D aniel bumped his head on the toilet wall and what a thump it was!

Rebecca Herbison (9)
Groggan Primary School

The Playground

When the bell rings
All the children are rushing up and down
Children playing on the hopscotch.

P1s and 2s in the shady garden
Children studying nature
Other children in their dens.

Ring-ting-ring goes the bell
Chatter, chatter, children go
Rushing to the line.

Rachel Clarke (9)
Groggan Primary School

In The Playground

In the playground I can see . . .
Fights going on.
The teachers are in the staffroom getting tea.
I can hear birds singing
and children shouting.
Trees shiver in the cold.

Andrew Rainey (8)
Groggan Primary School

In The Playground

The playground is a good place.
Everybody is happy.
Playing games.
People talking.
All the teachers are inside having tea.
Children eating their lunches.
You can hear children running.
Sometimes you can hear the wind.

Mark McMullen (9)
Groggan Primary School

In The Playground

When the bells start to ring
We all rush outside!
'Yippee!' some boys shout
As they start to play.
Some children are playing hopscotch,
Others are playing horses,
Or some prefer a peaceful walk around the wildlife garden.

Teachers stay inside
And gossip all the time!
While sipping cups of coffee
Marking books as well.
Talking about their students.
Oh, how boring teachers are.
Chat! Chat! Chat!

Katherine Aiken (9)
Groggan Primary School

A Monster In The Playground

In the playground
Children running
Happy faces all around
But all of a sudden
A monster pops out
But pops out of where?
Some don't know it's there
Until they start screaming
The monster tries to catch
A scared little boy
But then there's a bell
Ringing so loudly
The monster disappears
But where?
No one knows where.

Alana Nicholl (10)
Groggan Primary School

Senses

I like the sound of birds
Singing in the garden
I like the sound of cats
Miaowing at my knees
I like to see the boys fighting
Around all the teachers
I like to see the sun
Rising in the sky
I like to taste roast potatoes
Crunching in my mouth
I like to taste the ice cream
Cooling down my mouth
I like to touch the sand
Smooth in my hand
I like to touch the rabbits
Their fur is so soft
I like to smell the flowers
Swinging in the breeze
I like the smell of perfume
It smells very nice.

Danielle Winter (8)
Groggan Primary School

The Playground

In the playground I can see . . .
Children playing in the garden.
Coats left on the steps.
Children playing games.
Children falling on the pavement.
People walking on the steps.
Children playing horses and ponies.
Children running everywhere.

Rachael Kenny (8)
Groggan Primary School

The Playground

When the bell rings I run outside
To place a game
When I see a child all alone
I go and play with them
When I see somebody crying
I try to sort them out
When they stop I go on and play
When I see somebody shouting
I go over and calm them down
And ask them, 'Do you want to play?'
I go into the garden and see if everything is okay
I play horses with them
The playground is such fun.

Leagh Purdy (9)
Groggan Primary School

The Playground

When the bell rings,
We rush outside.
Some teachers come out
To supervise.

In the playground,
Children chatter.
Some fall to the ground,
With a clatter.

When the wildlife garden
Comes to life,
Birds start to sing
And build their nests.

Emma Johnston (9)
Groggan Primary School

The Playground

T he bell has rung so we all walk out.
H eaps of heavy children rushing to play whatever game they want.
E very sound I hear, like birds and children.

P laying children having fun, jumping, skipping.
L ots of laughter, talking and chatting,
A ll in groups, let's play again.
Y our friends will always play with you.
G oing round, jumping, skipping, playing games.
R owing children, what a fuss!
O n the hopscotch, *hop, hop, hop.*
U nhappy people as they fall to the ground.
'N o playing in the muck,' says the caretaker.
D own the dip now to catch them all.

Kirsty Wallace (8)
Groggan Primary School

The Playground

From the playground you can see,
The wildlife garden and maybe a bumblebee.
In the garden there are benches,
Bird feeders, pansies and primroses,
Daffodils and daisies.

In the playground you can hear
The children that the supervisors can't bear.
Falling and crying happens all the time.

When the whistle blows,
We all rush inside for lunch
Once we've finished we all run outside
To the noisy playground once again.

Carla Cameron (8)
Groggan Primary School

Senses

I like the sound of birds
Singing in a tree
I like the taste of ice cream
Cooling my tongue
I like the feeling of the sea
Tickling my toes
I like to see the sunset
In the afternoon
I like to smell the flowers
Swinging in the breeze
I like the sound of cars
Zooming past
I like the taste of chips
Sizzling in my mouth
I like to feel cats' and dogs' fur
For it is soft
I like to see dogs
Chasing after a ball
I like to smell the flowers
On a summer's day.

Chloe McKee (8)
Groggan Primary School

In The Playground

I walk outside and hear the birds singing
A lovely little tune!
I see my friends playing a game.
The teachers having a conversation in the staffroom.
I see my friends pointing at me
'Come over here and play with us.'
I hear the sounds of cars going by
As if they were two hundred lorries!
I see some people making friends
As if they always had known one another.

Nicole Cameron (8)
Groggan Primary School

Senses

I like the taste of ice cream
Lovely and sweet
I like to taste sweets
That everybody loves
I like to smell chips
In the chip pan
I like to smell fresh air
On a sunny day
I like to touch a dog
With its soft fur
I like to touch conkers
Lovely and smooth.

Adam Clarke (7)
Groggan Primary School

My Senses Poem

I like the taste of chicken
Going around my mouth.
I like the smell of popcorn
Popping on my nose.
I like the feel of cats
Tickling my hand.
I like the look of birds
Flying around the sky.

David Speedy (8)
Groggan Primary School

Senses

I like to touch a steering wheel on a car
I like to see racing cars on the track.
I like to smell sausages in the pan.
I like to taste Chinese down the town.
I like to hear the tractor working on the farm.

Denver Mills (7)
Groggan Primary School

Senses

I like the taste of cold ice cream
Going in my mouth

I like to hear bands
Rocking and rolling

I like to see medals
In my hands

I like to feel soft cats
Sliding up and down

I like to smell the dinner
Cooking on the stove.

Steven Thompson (7)
Groggan Primary School

Senses

I like to hear the sound
of the waves
crashing on the rocks
I like to feel the sand
tickling my feet at the beach
I like to see dogs
zooming after a ball
I like to taste ice cream
melting in my mouth.

Laura Coulter (7)
Groggan Primary School

The Playground

The playground is a place to run.
The games are filled with lots of fun.
It's the best time of the day
If we want to laugh and play.

Thomas Allen (9)
Groggan Primary School

Playground Bully

I sat in the playground very still,
When my friend came and sat beside me
Her name was Jill.
'What are you doing my little mate,
Sitting here all alone, you could be late.'
Suddenly I heard the fear of all my fears.
A deep rumbling going straight through my ears.
'Help, he's coming, the bully,' I cried.
And through my little eyes I spied
The massive bully with his leather coat on
With his studded boots covered in frog spawn.
He was coming towards me, I was full of alarm.
I started to run but he caught my arm.
He grabbed me by the scruff of the neck
And started to take everything,
Out of my pockets and everywhere,
Till I stood there with nothing to spare.
Fortunately, the bell rang.
The bully then ran, not turning back,
Straight to the line.

I followed in despair!

Adam McIlmoyle (10)
Groggan Primary School

The Playground

Outside, oh outside, in the big playground!
Children laughing, some crying.
Some tall, some small and some in-between.

Children playing 'catches' or playing on the hopscotch.
All having a good time.

Kids playing, running and chattering.
(Chat! Chat! Chat! Chat! Chat!)

Victoria Graham (9)
Groggan Primary School

In The Playground

In the playground I play
What do I play?
I play horses
It is such fun
But the bell rings for lunch
We really quickly munch
Go back out in a bunch
Out and over the jumps I go!
The playground's like a fairground
And we play happily all lunchtime long
Then the big, bad bell rings
In it is for work not play
Maths, English, science, then it's time to go home
And ride the real horse
After homework, of course.

Kathryn Cameron (11)
Groggan Primary School

Senses

I like to hear my fish
Blob, blob, blob

I like to taste my sausages
Sizzling on my tongue

I like to feel my chips
When I eat them

I like to see Nemo, Dorey, Marvin
Going into their castle

I like to smell different flowers
All different colours.

Sophie Millar (8)
Groggan Primary School

Senses

I like the sound of the waves
Crashing on the sand

I like the sound of Rebekah
Telling us a story

I like the taste of ice cream
Lovely in my mouth

I like to see the horses
Running in their field

I like to see everybody
Walking up and down

I like the touch of Rebekah
Her skin as soft as a kitten

I like to touch books
Sometimes they are smooth

I like the smell of perfume
Made from a flower

I like the smell of soap
It smells like lilies.

Hannah Brown (7)
Groggan Primary School

My Senses

I like to hear the sea
Crashing on the shore
I like to taste ice cream
On a sunny day
I like to feel the petals
On a flower
I like to see the sunset
Scatter away
I like to smell the flowers
On a summer's day.

Laura Agnew (8)
Groggan Primary School

My First Day At School

I walked in the gate to see,
A very big school,
Then I saw a playground,
A swimming pool, it was so cool!
There were monkey bars and little cars,
Big, tall towers and climbing frames.

Then came the school,
Banging doors and creaking floors,
I ran on up the corridor to my classroom,
It was a bad room, I hated it,
It was horrible.

(That was my first day at school.)

Rebecca Gregg (10)
Groggan Primary School

Senses

I like to touch dogs' fur;
It is soft.

I like the taste of sausages
Because they are nice.

I love the sound of the sea
Crashing on the rocks.

I can smell the smoke in the air
Going up my nose.

I can see my quad in my garage
With the light on.

Michael Craig (8)
Groggan Primary School

My Dream Playground!

Candy canes,
Climbing frames,
Lots of fun and games.

Monkey bars,
Big tall towers,
Lots of lovely flowers.

No more books,
Famous cooks,
It doesn't matter about your looks.

Bright balloons,
Great cartoons,
Cool tunes.

There's a chocolate pool
That's cool!
I really, really love my school.

Amy Wallace (10)
Groggan Primary School

My Playground Poem

In the playground we can shout
And we all can run about
On the swings we go so high
Until we nearly reach the sky.

In the playground we have such fun
Lying about in the sun
But then the old bell will ring
And we all shall rush right in!

Rachel Johnston (11)
Groggan Primary School

Playground Scare

Oh, why won't they
Let me pass?
I've been waiting here
So long
It's like waiting for the church bell
To go *ding-dong!*

They must be giants
Those ones
So big and tall
I'm really scared of them
Especially when
They're kicking a ball.

Now they're helping me
In my class
And I think I'm their
Little lass
They help me when I'm sore,
So I'm not
Scared of them
Anymore.

Shannon Cameron (11)
Groggan Primary School

The Little Boy

He's as scared as a mouse
Does he live in a house?
He sits in the chestnut tree
Come on, play on the ground.
He's normally watching me
Whilst I play my games with Bill and James
He's always there to see my friend and me
Why doesn't he come out from behind that tree?

Taylor-Ann Black (11)
Groggan Primary School

Senses

I like the sound of the sea
Crashing up the beach.

I like the taste of ice cream
Making my mouth freeze.

I like to touch my cat's fluff
Tickling my hand.

I like to see my cat Ginger
Playing on the grass.

I like to smell roses
Growing in my garden.

I like the sound of singing
Tickling my ears.

I like the taste of sausages
Sizzling in my mouth.

I like to touch warm water
On a cold day.

I like to see butterflies
All around me.

I like to smell perfume
On my mum
Ruth.

Ruth McKeown (8)
Groggan Primary School

Senses

I like to see the sweet birds in the trees.
I like to feel the soft dogs.
I like to hear my mum.
I like to taste McDonald's.
I like to touch my dog.

Nicky Black (9)
Groggan Primary School

Fantastic Day At School

We will scream and shout
As we run about
Up and down the climbing frame
Oh what a good game!
Oh what fun it is
To go on that ride outside
Down the waterslide
Everyone screaming with excitement.

Ileanna McDowell (11)
Groggan Primary School

The First Day Of School

Out the door the horror came
People that were lame
People that were fast
People that wore casts
Away the horrors went
I made a friend called Kent
Kent and I are so happy
So I couldn't be more happy.

Jonathan McIlroy (9)
Groggan Primary School

Playground Poem

In the playground where I play
I wish that I could stay all day
But the bell has gone
We must go in
The whole school makes such a din.

Back in class I mess about
My horrible teacher, he won't let me out.

Stephanie French (11)
Groggan Primary School

The Race

We were on the line
Ready to go
Dale, James, Adam
And me
Then the whistle went
And we were off.

First it was James
Then it was Adam
After, was Dale
Then it was me
We were speeding
Down the playground.

At once James fell
And Adam tripped over
Dale didn't see
And fell *splat!*
On the ground.

I had to do something
I skipped around
I could see
The finish line.

I was on my way
To all the glory
I leapt over the line
I couldn't believe my luck
For I was the champion of the world!

Philip Smyth (10)
Groggan Primary School

My Playground Dreams!

In the playground in my dreams,
There are monkey bars,
Climbing towers.

In the classroom
There are dancing games
And some candy canes.

In the dinner hall
There are tons of buns.

In the school
There's a pool,
It's very cool.

In the PE hall
I play with a ball,
The PE teacher is very tall.

Chloe Buick (9)
Groggan Primary School

The Best School In The World

The best school in the world is my school,
A football pitch, a hockey pitch and a swimming pool as well,
Inside, a sweetie shop, a pick'n'mix, no work is done at all.

The teachers, they are crazy about this mad, mad school,
The headmaster, Mr Scott, his patience goes up the wall.
The council built this school because the children were complaining.

I think this is a good idea although I don't know anything.
I mean look at this writin', it's horrible, I cannot *spel a ting!*

The school motto is we all have fun,
We learn and play together,
We like our school,
We love our school,
It's the best school in the world.

Victoria Bond (10)
Groggan Primary School

My Senses

I like the taste of spaghetti
In the saucepan.
I like the sound of a snooker ball
Flying into the pot.
I like the touch of my cat;
It is so soft.
I like to see a tractor
Ploughing the field.
I like the smell of bacon
In the pan.

Andrew Hamill (8)
Groggan Primary School

Manchester United

M idfield brilliant
A lways breaking transfer records
N ow who's got Rooney?
C 'mon United!
H einze, new defender for 12 million pounds
E ngland's top team!
S trikers are the best in the world
T rophies are always being won!
E very other team, *beware!*
R onaldo, a great buy at 12 million pounds

U nhappy that they lost but we'll bounce back
N obody is better than Manchester United!
I ce-cool tricks done by Ronaldo
T oo good for the other team!
E veryone knows the famous Old Trafford
D efence is absolutely brilliant.

James Freeman (11)
Kilmoyle Primary School

Eagles

Eagles
My favourite birds
Flying like rockets
Fast and furious
Landing like aeroplanes.

Eagles
Their sharp claws
Slicing their prey
Tearing off flesh
Catching mice and rabbits.

Eagles
King of birds
Moving silently
Hovering in circles
Golden-brown feathers.

I do like eagles.

Kurtis Ashcroft (10)
Kilmoyle Primary School

Superheroes

They have got mega abilities
Like super agility
Invisibility
Hyper-sharp razors
Eye-beam lasers
Super strength
Arms stretch to incredible length
Control weather
Float like a feather
They're a hit
And I think that's it.

Sam Kane (11)
Kilmoyle Primary School

Mount Vesuvius

Suddenly there was a great rumble
Mount Vesuvius had erupted!

People started running for their lives
Trying to beat the steaming hot lava
It caught up, melted their flesh,
Covered them in hot ashes.

The sight was so awful
Seeing smoke, flames, lakes of lava
Helpless people hardened to stone
And terror in the crowd.

The volcano caused death and misery
I will never forget that day!

Naomi Bleakly (9)
Kilmoyle Primary School

Farming

I like tractors.
The big, powerful, pulling kind.
The bright coloured, loud, fast kind.
I do like tractors.

I like cows.
The fat, chubby, tame kind.
The black and white, furry kind.
I do like cows.

I like farming.
The hardworking, fun kind.
The feeding calves, driving tractors kind.
I do like farming.

David Miskelly (11)
Kilmoyle Primary School

Unicorns

I like unicorns
The beautiful fluffy kind
With their pearly-white horns
And their golden hooves
Oh, I do like unicorns!

I love unicorns
The way they gallop
Like doves in the sky
With silver tails
And silky fur
Oh, I do love unicorns!

Magical, majestic
And perfect
How they fly in the moonlit sky
Exciting, riding high in the starry sky
Oh, I do like unicorns!

Unicorns are just so lovely
Oh, I do love unicorns!

Laura Freeman (9)
Kilmoyle Primary School

Planes And Motorbikes

I like planes
The easy to fly kind
The two-winged planes
The floating kind
I like planes.

I like motorbikes
The rubber-burning kind
The skidding kind
The high horsepower kind
I like motorbikes.

James McLaughlin (11)
Kilmoyle Primary School

Arsenal

A rsenal, hot, on fire, the greatest
R unning quickly, scoring fantastic goals
S houting, singing, they've scored a goal
E normous new stadium called Ashgrove
N il, the score for the other team
A rsene Wenger, the top manager
L junberg scores like a torpedo.

That's Arsenal!

Kris Purdy (10)
Kilmoyle Primary School

Luis Saha

L iking Luis as I do.
U nder control of Sir Alex.
I ntercepting a player and scoring.
S triker is his position.

S ir Alex is his manager.
A ugust 8th is his birthday.
H ating Liverpool as he does.
A n amazing star for United.

Charles Stewart (10)
Kilmoyle Primary School

Dogs

I like dogs
The fluffy, gentle, quiet kind
The lovely, lively, playful kind
Take it for a walk kind
Bath it in some water kind
Dry it when you're done kind
I do like dogs.

Nikita Kane (10)
Kilmoyle Primary School

Volcanoes

Volcanoes
Rumbling and banging
Exploding
Rivers of lava
Running down the land.

Volcanoes
Like a lion roaring
Vulcan the Roman god
Hammering on the iron
A great fear among people.

Volcanoes
Lighting like sparklers
Terror in the people's eyes
Molten rock dripping down
Red-hot lava burning people's skin.

Volcanoes
Great fear comes from the volcanoes.
Do you fear them?
The death of plants and trees and people
The great, angry volcanoes!

Harry McKeown (9)
Kilmoyle Primary School

Ponies

I like ponies.
The lovely, soft, furry kind.
The fast, speedy kind.
Ride them over jumps.
Groom their bodies, manes and tails.
I do love ponies.

Nicola Cochrane (10)
Kilmoyle Primary School

My Brother

My brother
Robert
Seven years old
Brown eyes
Brown hair
My brother

My brother
Loves to play
With cars
Listen to music
Play hide-and-seek
My brother

Oh brother
You annoy me
In my room
At school
Taking my sweets
My brother

My brother
Hates school
And homework
But loves
Drawing
My brother.

Elizabeth Morrow (9)
Kilmoyle Primary School

Volcanoes

Mount St Helens
Booming
Roaring
Sizzling
Bang
The volcano strikes again!

Mount Vesuvius
Rumbling
Poisonous gas
Screams
Crash
The volcano strikes again!

Mount Etna
Waves of lava
Melting flesh
Bodies dropping
Destruction
The volcano strikes again!

Mount Fuji
Lava bubbling
Havoc
Terror in their eyes
Flames of devastation
The volcano strikes again!

Mount Pelee
Hot molten rock
People choking
Lava oozing
Misery all around
The volcano strikes again!

Hannah Rose Kirkpatrick (10)
Kilmoyle Primary School

Snow

Snow
Falling
Fluttering and freezing
Sparkling and shining.

Snow
Playing
Snowballs and sleighs
Snowmen and icicles.

Snow
Melting
Slushy and icy
Skidding and sliding.

Jordan Christie (10)
Kilmoyle Primary School

Fireworks

Fireworks, fireworks, big and small
The rocket is the best one of all
I watch as they go up into the sky
Then look up and see the colour die.

Red ones, blue and lots more
I watch them while I sit by the door.
The sparks turn and twirl round and round
Then slowly fall to the ground.

I watch until they are all done out
And then I go home
And wait another year
Until the fireworks are back here.

Ryan McAuley (10)
St Comgall's Primary School, Antrim

An Autumn Day

The wind is howling,
The leaves are falling,
It means only one thing,
It's autumn.

Autumn leaves,
Brown, rusty-red,
Sunny yellow,
Sparkling orange,
All falling like one big herd,
Tumbling, dancing parachuting
And piling to the ground.

The gentle sound of leaves
Crunching
As I walk past,
The green and brown acorns falling
And conkers too,
Children playing happily
On
An autumn day!

Siobhan McQuillan (11)
St Comgall's Primary School, Antrim

Happiness Is . . .

Going out with your friends,
Telling jokes about funny things,
Coming home on a warm summer's night,
Sleeping all night,
Getting up in the morning,
My mum making lunch,
And then off to school
For another educational day.

Ciaran O'Hara (10)
St Comgall's Primary School, Antrim

Titanic

In 1912 our beautiful liner set sail,
The winds, they were calm,
Not blowing a gale,
All on board were excited and glad,
Not knowing that later,
It would all end so sad.
Across the Atlantic the air, cold and eerie,
The man on the lookout,
Saw the icebergs so clearly,
But too late now to worry,
Nothing he could do,
The fate was sealed for passengers and crew.
At midnight the unsinkable liner went down
And all but 800 people did drown!
It now rests on a seabed,
But the story lives on,
About the voyage of Titanic,
And why it went wrong.

Anthony Devlin (11)
St Comgall's Primary School, Antrim

Break Time

Sitting in my chair,
Sweat pouring off my face,
My own tensions building,
The bell rings, *bling! Bling!*
Charging out to play
People playing football,
Skipping, shouting,
Suddenly the bell rings,
We come in and sit down,
We're prisoners till 12.30!

Matthew Montgomery (11)
St Comgall's Primary School, Antrim

Golden Waterfall

Autumn is a colourful waterfall
Collecting shiny conkers
A big rustic haul
Getting ready for the darker days.

Animals hibernate
Jack Frost is coming
Birds migrate
The fog is looming close.

Crunchy leaves
Red, bronze, fiery colours
Bare trees
The colder days are coming.

Stars in the sky,
Brown, crunchy acorns
Fiery leaves lie
Hedgehogs sleep
And badgers do too.

Shannon Connor (11)
St Comgall's Primary School, Antrim

Happiness Is . . .

Happiness is . . .
Playing my favourite computer game, The Sims 2,
Having a brilliant time with my best friends,
Going to have a good look in modern shops,
Playing the PlayStation2, The Sims Bustin' Out,
Chilling out on a Saturday night,
Having a good laugh, eating lots of chocolate.
Having a good lie in bed on a Sunday morning,

That's what
Happiness
Is!

Niamh O'Connor (11)
St Comgall's Primary School, Antrim

Break Time!

Sitting in class
Waiting anxiously
Ten minutes to go
Cannot stop looking at the clock.

The bell rings
I race to the door
My heart beating fast
Freedom at last!

Air blowing in my face
Happily playing
Skipping and playing football
A shadow overcasts us.

The bell rings again
I line up
Lots of work awaits me
All I can hear is
Moan, moan and moan.
Danielle!

Danielle O'Kane (11)
St Comgall's Primary School, Antrim

An Autumn Walk

A walk through the park,
A taste of autumn leaves,
There are beautiful colours,
Swaying in the breeze,
Rusty-red and copper-brown,
Like a burning fire,
Twinkling in the distance,
The crackling and the crunching,
Dancing and piling,
All on an autumn walk.

Gemma McErlane (10)
St Comgall's Primary School, Antrim

Vikings, Vikings Invade

Vikings steal
And Vikings raid
Vikings have a blood raid
Vikings, Vikings invade.

They steal precious treasures
And slaughter people
Using victims for slaves
Vikings, Vikings invade.

They bring shields and chain mail
They carry axes in their hands
Vikings, Vikings invade.

The Vikings travel in longships
Ready to take over the villages
People scream
Vikings, Vikings invade!

Chloe Langton (10)
St Comgall's Primary School, Antrim

An Autumn Day

Leaves are twirling round and round
All they make is a rustling sound
They are all different colours but the best is ruby-red
Just as the wind stops, they get to their bed.

When the birds start to migrate
The animals get ready to hibernate
Bronze and amber leaves are also nice
Then we will go to the frost and the ice.

All the leaves have fallen off the trees
So then we will have a really cool breeze
Now we are all going to sneeze
And then we will watch all the trees freeze.

Rebecca Kennedy (10)
St Comgall's Primary School, Antrim

The Storm

The sky went dark
You could hear the sound of wind banging in your eardrum,
The trees creaking at breaking point,
Belting rain hitting against your face,
Like someone slapping over and over.
Boats getting thrashed on the shores,
Water taking over, hitting the windows on my house,
Going so fast they shatter.
Everyone grabbing hold of something so they won't blow away.
So much mass destruction left behind,
The world can't bear another storm again.

Mollie Somers (11)
St Comgall's Primary School, Antrim

Hush Now My Baby

The baby awakes and it's my turn.
As I walk into the room,
My baby's smile begins to bloom
But when I turn to walk away,
Baby starts to weep!
And I think to myself,
Please, please, go to sleep!
So I pick her up in my arms
My baby starts to work her charms!
All is peaceful but I spoke
Too soon!

Alexandra McDonnell (11)
St Comgall's Primary School, Antrim

A Sleepless Night

Hush now baby, here I am,
That's it, go back to sleep,
Tiptoe out, oh no, there's a toy,
Oh come on then, back in my arms.

Walking around the room,
Toys are shaken,
Bottle is sucked,
Everything is tried.

Yes, finally he's asleep,
Out I tiptoe,
Don't tell me that's another toy.

Sophie Mahon (10)
St Comgall's Primary School, Antrim

Autumn Poem

Leaves falling off every tree.
Golden, brown and peach leaves falling.
The spiky conker shells rotting away.
The days getting dark and darker every day.

The leaves swirling in the air.
The animals getting ready for hibernation.
The leaves being crunched by everyone.

The leaves being scattered, it's just like a sea of leaves.
Birds migrating to another country.
The rustle and bustle of the leaves.

Natilla Lane (11)
St Comgall's Primary School, Antrim

Titanic Terror

Titanic tickets sold fast
People shoving and bumping to get on
It's like a palace on water
A floating mansion.

Frederick Fleet sees an iceberg
His calls are too late
The crashing and banging
The once great ship is sinking.

The frantic struggles of the people
The rumbling roar of the ship
There has been destruction and devastation
People determined to get off.

Screaming children, fathers left behind
Calling California!
Many lives have been lost at sea
On April 14th 1912.

The Titanic was once the great
Ship of dreams.

Ben Johnston (10)
St Comgall's Primary School, Antrim

Seasons

Spring is the first season
When things start to grow

Summer is the second season
When the sun will brightly glow

Autumn is the third season
When leaves fall to the ground

Winter is the last of all
When snow falls all around.

Paul Joyce (10)
St Comgall's Primary School, Antrim

School

When I was five I started to school
I really loved it then
I learned to read and do my sums
Though I never used a pen.

Then as the years went slowly by
The work got really tough
I really don't like this, I thought
It's not my kind of stuff.

So many things to learn
And many tests to do
The teachers shouting, 'Hurry up,
I can't wait all day for you.'

It was great when sports day came along
We all went raving mad
We'd run and scream and jump and fall
And no one was ever sad.

Now I'm moving to a bigger school
Where there's no more fun and games
So many teachers every day
I'll never remember their names.

Dearbháile Liddy (10)
St Comgall's Primary School, Antrim

The Sea Behaves In Many Ways

The sea behaves in many ways
As calm as a puddle of rain
So gentle you can see the fish
It smells like the great outdoors.

The sea behaves in many ways
So rough it lashes against the rocks
It is as bad as the 'Hulk',
Or maybe as bad as 'Godzilla'!

Pol McElligott (10)
St Comgall's Primary School, Antrim

I Am A Grape

A sour green grape
Waiting in the supermarket
To be chosen.

I'm covered in plastic
And on a shelf
I have lots of friends and family
I'm not by myself.

Someone is coming
They have picked my bag
I am getting pushed about in a car.

Suddenly the car stops
And a door opens
I'm put on a shelf again
My bag is opening . . .
A man is eating me.

Ahhh!

Shannen Dilworth (9)
St Comgall's Primary School, Antrim

Loneliness

Loneliness is sad.
On the day they leave you.
No people there beside you.
Eating without you.
Love is no longer in the air.

I don't want to live without you.
Nothing is there anymore.
I would not want to be without you.
I loved him very much.
He broke my heart.

Natasha McMahon (10)
St Comgall's Primary School, Antrim

I Am An Apple

I am an apple
A juicy red apple
hanging on a tree
waiting and waiting
for someone to pick me.

All of my friends
are picked or eaten
that's what scares me
hanging on this tree.

My father and mother
were thrown away
just because they
were old as day.

Now here are people
coming for me
wonder what they
will do to me?

Ciara Dilworth (9)
St Comgall's Primary School, Antrim

Friends

Friends are fun to have,
They're with you every day,
A knock on the door
And they're out to play,
Friends are important to you and me.

Friends are the best things in the world,
They are there when you're feeling down,
When you're on your own
They are there on the double,
Friends are the ones you want to have.

Tara Wilson (9)
St Comgall's Primary School, Antrim

The Farm

In summertime we went to a farm,
The baby goat, it bit my arm,
It wasn't sore, it was just a nip,
I just grinned and bit my lip.

Then we fed the baby lamb,
I couldn't believe it,
His name was 'Sam'!

We fed the chickens and the hens,
We threw the food into the pens.
Next we came to a great big pig,
It looked as if it had a wig!

Then we went for a nice long walk,
Out of the bushes came a beautiful peacock.
Its feathers were red, green and blue,
Some yellow, brown and purple too.

We had a great day, I have to say,
I hope we can go back some other day!

Shannon Close (9)
St Comgall's Primary School, Antrim

Holidays

H olidays are lots of fun.
O ut on your holiday with no school
L ove all the water parks
I ce cream, yummy!
D evines, we're in America
A musements with lots of dolphins.
Y ummy chips and burgers
S hopping - yippee!

Ciara Devine (10)
St Comgall's Primary School, Antrim

The Prayer Of The Vicious Dog

Dear God,
I pray this day for meat and bones
Please give me some peace.
I wish for a best friend
And a bed for those lazy dreams.

I hope it rains with dog food
Chicken, turkey and fish.
I wish for a great big china plate
Instead of a dirty dish.

But God, the thing I really want
Apart from all that stuff above
Is somebody who cares about me
And gives me lots of love.
                              Amen.

Dermot Mullin (10)
St Comgall's Primary School, Antrim

Viking Warriors

Viking warriors
In the boat they go
Travelling in all storms
Even through the snow
Getting ready, on our way
The people will have to pray
Get out the swords ready to slay
On the shore
And ready to fight
Almost night
Here we come
Children screaming
Running scared.

Nathan McGarry (9)
St Comgall's Primary School, Antrim

Awake At Night

Awake at night
The shadows in the dark
Look very scary until dawn's first light.

I feel very frightened all night
Alone in the dark
Such a fright.

Shadows through my window
What could they be?
Very creepy - I need to wee!
They look like big cherries and berries
They keep tapping on my window
Shadows playing a game of limbo.

The door is creaking and the floorboards too -
I find out that it is my toys
And my brother trying to scare me . . . phew!

Martin Gourley (9)
St Comgall's Primary School, Antrim

Awake At Night

One stormy night
I woke with a fright
I saw a ghost all dressed in white.
I went back to sleep.
It was very cold
I called Mum and Dad
They said, 'Go to sleep.'
I saw the car light shine
Like a bulb.
In the back, my dogs were barking
It scared me a lot.
My dad came in and told me to go to sleep.

David Quinn (10)
St Comgall's Primary School, Antrim

Fireworks

F ireworks, fireworks, fireworks
I love fireworks, the way they crackle and *bang!*
R ockets and bangers are all I can hear
E very firework gets louder and louder
W ow! Big Catherine wheels in the sky
O h how I love the colours in the sky
R emember they are very dangerous
K ids love watching them
S ad when they are all over.

Bronagh Lavery (9)
St Comgall's Primary School, Antrim

The Prayer Of The Little Rabbit

Dear God,
Give us food to feed on
Give us a nice safe hutch where we can live
Let us have sun not rain
To keep us warm
Give us lots of juicy orange carrots to eat.
Amen.

Chloe Todd (10)
St Comgall's Primary School, Antrim

The Prayer Of The Little Tiger

Dear God,
Let the rivers be full of water to drink
Give us lots of animals to eat
Give us lots of trees to get shade under
Protect us from all hunters
Protect us from being captured for the zoo
Give me a family of tiger cubs
And a cave to live in.

Amen.

Aaron Geoghegan (10)
St Comgall's Primary School, Antrim

During The Night

During the night
I wake up
Crash
Who's there?
Boom!
Get up
Great big shadow
Bump!
Go downstairs
Look down
Oh, it's only a mouse!

Lee Mason (9)
St Comgall's Primary School, Antrim

My Pet Rabbit

My rabbit is called Snowy.
He is white and fluffy
and soft like a teddy bear.
He loves to be stroked
and given cuddles
and best of all,
he's my pet rabbit.

Callum McAteer (8)
St Comgall's Primary School, Antrim

The Prayer Of The Little Rabbits

Dear God,
Give us more delicious vegetables to nibble on
And more cosy straw to sleep in.
Give us plenty of rabbit food
And protect us from all dogs and cats.

                                Amen.

Rebecca Moore (9)
St Comgall's Primary School, Antrim

Football

I like football
Because I am not tall
I like football
Because I am small

When I score
I just want more
When I score
I roll on the floor

I like football
Because I am quick
I like football
Because I have a good kick

When I am in the nets
People are making bets
That I will not save the goals
In-between the two big, white poles.

Karl Thompson (9)
St Comgall's Primary School, Antrim

Rabbits Have . . .

A twitchy nose that goes up and down.
Long ears that flap
Bushy tail like a fluffy ball
Blinking eyes like a door opening and closing
Fluffy fur like a woolly coat.

Rabbits can be . . .
Wild
Kept as pets
Big or small.

Nicole Quinn (9)
St Comgall's Primary School, Antrim

I Love Football

I play football all the time
football is always on my mind.
In my house the ball hits the door
I head, shoot, dribble and score.

I am going to the match at eight,
me, my dad and my best mate.
I hope one day to play at Windsor Park
on a dark and rainy night.

But first I must get my homework done
oh no, this isn't too much fun!

Gareth Rainey (9)
St Comgall's Primary School, Antrim

My Dog

I have a dog
she is called Amy.
At night in the house,
she gets very lazy.
She goes for a walk
during the day
and every chance she gets
she plays in the hay.
Her colour is black,
her collar is red
and when she gets tired
she goes to her bed.

My dog Amy.

Ryan Bevin (9)
St Comgall's Primary School, Antrim

Seasons

Spring . . .
the baby lambs jump and play,
to celebrate the first spring day.

Summer . . .
follows without a doubt,
as cherry blossom begins to sprout.

Autumn . . .
rears its chilly head,
to bring stormy wind and rain instead.

Winter . . .
brings a cool surprise
of bitter chills and snow-laden skies.

Conor Logue (8)
St Comgall's Primary School, Antrim

Dogs

Dogs are cheeky little things.
They like to steal your golden rings.
When you take them out for walks
they sniff between the trees.
They bark and bark, run and pull
until you let them free.
They are joyful, cute and kind
and as happy as can be.
Dogs don't huff and dogs don't shout,
they love you as you are.
Just keep taking them for lots of walks
because they'll never drive a car.

Aoife Marley (9)
St Comgall's Primary School, Antrim

My Pet Fish

My pet fish live in a dish
Speedy swims in water
Just like an otter
Bob has a job
That's to keep up with Speedy
Speedy is strong
But Bob's a little bit weedy
Either way, they're still
My pet fish
And they are so much fun.

Connor Keenan (8)
St Comgall's Primary School, Antrim

My Little Dragon

My little dragon, he woke me up one day
He dragged me down the stairs
He wanted me to play.
He chased me up and down the hall
When I got into the kitchen
He was climbing up the wall.
He sat down on the table
And ate pancakes off a plate
I sat on a chair thinking
Of the things that he would hate.
Suddenly I jumped up, in a terrible way
Did this all really happen
Or did my mind float away?

Ruairi McPoland (9)
St Joseph's Primary School, Dunloy

The 11+ Results

I woke up that morning
And could hear my mother roaring.
'Get up for the results.'
Oh no! My head was in a twist
And I was feeling rather sick.
I looked at that slip
And do you know what I had . . .
Well let's just say it wasn't bad.

Ryan Kennedy (11)
St Joseph's Primary School, Dunloy

Feelings

Some days you could be sad.
Some days you could be mad.
Some days you could feel drowsy,
Exhausted, tired and weary.
Some days you could be cheerless,
Depressed, heartbroken and careless.
Some days you could be blissful,
Laughing, light-hearted and joyful.
You have different feelings every day.
You feel sad or happy and mad or gay!

Nicola McShane (10)
St Joseph's Primary School, Dunloy

Fairies

Magical fairies sparkling so bright,
In the sky like a twinkling light.
Blue fairies, yellow fairies, pink fairies, white,
Make me feel contented in the darkness of night.
If only I were a fairy too,
I'd feel so happy just like they do.

Catherine McDaid (10)
St Joseph's Primary School, Dunloy

Scrambler

S cramblers are cool, scramblers are fast.
C oming down the track swerving and dodging.
R acing over the sand dunes and across the desert.
A ppreciating the help the wind was giving me.
M aking the dust rise behind me as I go fast.
B ystanders are cheering loudly as I go past.
L osing the other riders as I went out in front.
E verything was flashing past.
R ough pebbles scattered as I came to the finish line.

Keelan Harkin (11)
St Joseph's Primary School, Dunloy

Butterfly

B eautiful butterfly
U nder the beautiful flowers
T affeta wings flutter
T alk to me please!
E very other butterfly flies away from me
R ather you would not
F ly away from me
L ay down your taffeta wings and rest
Y ou'll be all right, I'll make sure!

Eimer McKendry (8)
St Joseph's Primary School, Dunloy

Playing Is . . .

Fun every day,
Laughing with my friends,
Skipping with ropes,
Running too fast,
Hide-and-seek,
Darting in and out,
Being with my friends.

Megan Kennedy (8)
St Joseph's Primary School, Dunloy

School

School is mostly a very lively place.
Sometimes so lively we might shout and talk the whole day.
The dinner is like a feast with sausages, chips and bacon.
But then there came the day
When the principal had to say
The school was closing down,
She said it with a big, sad frown.
But we couldn't help ourselves shouting,
'We want the school to stay!'

David O'Neill (11)
St Joseph's Primary School, Dunloy

My Granda

He had a John Deere, that no one went near.
The sound you could hear as it drove near.
For as sure as the seasons came round
Granda and his John Deere were sure to be found.
His number plate was out of date,
For only Granda could find it at the scrapyard gate.
I got to ride on that famous John Deere
Which I'll remember for many a year.

Shauna Draine (11)
St Joseph's Primary School, Dunloy

11+ Results

It's the morning of the results and you're feeling really sick.
You're worried and you're anxious and you hope it's over quick.
You go down to the kitchen and your mum makes you tea.
She reaches you the letter and says, 'Open it and see.'
You're flustered and you're jumpy and you're dreading this day.
You open up the letter and see you've got a ?

Annemarie Esler (11)
St Joseph's Primary School, Dunloy

A Day In My Life

Out through the garden
In through the gates
Off to school I really hate.
In we go to our little wooden desks
Oh how I dread for those Friday morning tests.
Into our bags and out with our books
It's not as bad as it really looks.
Ten out of ten and all's going well
Just as I hear the lunchtime bell.
Lunchtime's over, two hours to go.
Here comes the weekend and an end to my woe.

Nicole O'Neill (9)
St Joseph's Primary School, Dunloy

If I Were A Sports Car

If I were a sports car,
I would rev my engine
And all heads would turn to stare
At my sleek bodywork.
Dare to race me in the street?
I'd burn them off and honk my horn.
All the money in the world
Couldn't buy my cool looks.

Alastair Dooey (9)
St Joseph's Primary School, Dunloy

If I Were A Headmaster

If I were a headmaster I would ban maths in the classroom.
Have no teachers and play all day.
No more rubbish Friday tests to study all night for.
But just for now it's off to school.

Fearghal O'Boyle (8)
St Joseph's Primary School, Dunloy

My Wee Kitty

My wee kitty, is a wee bit nippy.
She always needs to go to the loo.
Whether we be in the car or at the Spar
Whether we be home or away or even at play
She always needs to go to the loo.
But for my wee kitty
It is a real pity
Her name is Lulu.

Stephen McToal (10)
St Joseph's Primary School, Dunloy

The Mirror

I can see a face
It's stumpy and all white
I can see a face
It's mine! Oh yes! All right!
I can see a face
With long brown hair and a nose
I can see a face
Oh yes! It's mine - now I know!

Kirstin Ingram (8)
St Joseph's Primary School, Dunloy

A Sports Car Is . . .

A sports car is . . .
A really fast car
A sports car is cool
Some sports cars have turbo
Some sports cars have a muffler
Some sports cars have powerful engines
Formula One cars are the fastest cars on Earth.

Niall Smyth (9)
St Joseph's Primary School, Dunloy

Butterfly

B rightly coloured little angel
U nable to stay still
T wirling round and round
T ucking up your feet as you fly
E legantly landing on the grass
R aising your colourful wings
F litting about restlessly
L ightly fluttering around
Y ou've lightened up my day.

Shannon Carey (9)
St Joseph's Primary School, Dunloy

Motorbike

M ean machine on the road
O ver steep hills we fly
T urbo sparks push us forward
O ut in the open, fresh and free
R allying along, roaring loud
B rakes screech as a corner looms
I nto the town, speed traps around
K eep moving on, head lowered down
E ven when the blue light flashes.

Leon Dillon (8)
St Joseph's Primary School, Dunloy

Animal

A renas for horses' hard work
N ettles don't sting them
I nsects they eat
M unching all day
A lonely thing then, now on to play
L ying down, they ran away.

Erin Kearns (9)
St Joseph's Primary School, Dunloy

Why Me?

Why pick on me?
What's wrong with me?
Is it my hair?
Is it my glasses?
Why me?

I'm sitting in the corner
I'm feeling really sad
I have no friends
To stand up for me
For when I'm feeling sad.

I don't want to tell the teacher
I don't want to tell my mum
Because if I do
I will get bullied again
And that's why I'm so afraid.

Why do they pick on me?

Laura McKeague (10)
St Joseph's Primary School, Dunloy

A Story Of The Underwater World

When the tide is out I hide in seaweed,
But sometimes I get caught in the net,
But when I do, I use my brain and use my small, strong claws.
But alas, here he comes,
The man with the two little thingies,
He captures me and brings me to the surface.
I fight with the lobster until I get chosen.
He picks me up and I counter attack.
He drops me and I decide to have a little fun.
I climb up people's legs and nip them where they don't like it.
So I go back to the sea,
My adventure is over, yep it is,
About me, the sly, mischievous little crab.

Thomas McCann (10)
St Joseph's Primary School, Dunloy

I Wish I Was A Vampire

I lie to my mum
She sends me to my room
I say to myself, 'I wish I was a vampire.'
Suddenly a shadow looms
I knew at once it was a vampire
A piercing scream escapes
I woke up and told Mum the news
She didn't believe but then she asked,
'What are those two little holes in your neck?'

Dean Boyle (9)
St Joseph's Primary School, Dunloy

Fishing

F ind a good place to stand,
I nsect on to the hook,
S it still and wait,
H old the rod tightly,
I magine what I will catch,
N ice and steady, reel it in,
G ood! It's a big one!

Daniel Henry (9)
St Joseph's Primary School, Dunloy

School Is . . .

School is a place where you have to do boring things
Like science and history
But I'd rather play football
Oh I wish there was no such thing as school
Oh I wish I was at home
I love my house, it's like a dream
Compared to school.

Morgan Lyttle (9)
St Joseph's Primary School, Dunloy

Horse Racing

How many horses in the race?
We have a good chance of winning.
Lining up at the starting gate.
I know we have a good chance.
This could be our lucky day.
Relax, loosen up the reins
And keep my head down.
The horse responds with a nod of her head.
Get ready, set, go!

Blaine McDaid (8)
St Joseph's Primary School, Dunloy

Rainbows

R ed is the colour that appears on the top
A nd violet is the last in the arc
I n the sky is where you can see them
N ot visible when it's night-time or dark
B elieved by some to lead to a treasure
O ver which the song says the bluebirds do fly
W hat am I talking about? You may ask
S ure, the answer is written down the side.

Aisling Crawford (9)
St Joseph's Primary School, Dunloy

Flowers

F lowers, flowers wonderful flowers.
L ovely, sweet, colourful flowers.
O range, blue, purple flowers.
W ild lavender is the best.
E very flower you wish for is there.
R ose petals can be red or pink.
S uch a lovely display of flowers.

Rachael Kearns (9)
St Joseph's Primary School, Dunloy

Butterfly

B utterfly, butterfly
U nder the green leaf
T op of the tree
T alk to me!
E ach butterfly isn't as beautiful as me
R onald is my name
F lying all around, come after me
L ike a submarine my colour is
Y ellow like a bee.

Aimie Scott (9)
St Joseph's Primary School, Dunloy

What's In A Rainbow?

R aspberries, red and juicy
A pples, green and sweet
I ce cream, white and cold
N oodles, yellow and wiggly
B uns, brown and chocolately
O ranges, juicy and delicious
W ater, blue and clear
    that's what I see!

Rachel O'Loan (8)
St Joseph's Primary School, Dunloy

Monkey

M onkey in the jungle,
O ver the trees it swings,
N ot a care in the world,
K nocking bananas off trees,
E njoying the thrill of swinging by its tail,
Y elling and screeching like a kid in the park.

Chantelle Smiley (8)
St Joseph's Primary School, Dunloy

Oh How I Wish To Be A Dolphin

If I was a dolphin
I would jump up really high
And make all the people
Think that I could fly

I would jump through the waves
All day and all night
And my light would
Be the moonlight bright

It would be a delight
To swim in the sea
But I'm really glad
To be *me!*

Aideen Brogan (11)
St Joseph's Primary School, Dunloy

Boredom

Sitting in class,
Science, English and maths.
Sleeping from nine to three.
I'm bored in school
The whole day through,
And please, what can I do?

Ronan Cunning (10)
St Joseph's Primary School, Dunloy

Snake

S lithers along the long, stony ground.
N ever loses its prey.
A lways on the move.
K ing of the reptiles.
E veryone is scared, because here comes the *snake!*

Ronan Martin (10)
St Joseph's Primary School, Dunloy

Football Fan

F ootball is a professional game.
O n the pitch you get a lot of fame.
O n the pitch you're sure to get a stitch.
T here's a boy on the pitch called Mitch.
B ellows and shouts, the crowd will yell.
A ll the team players are swell.
L anguage to the referee is not allowed.
L ater the crowd shout loud.

F orest Green stands no chance against us.
A nything bad makes the whole team mad.
N obody went home crying, because we won.

Caolan McIlfatrick (10)
St Joseph's Primary School, Dunloy

Bullying

B is for badness that hurts other people.
U is for when you're under their arm.
L is for being left alone.
L is for loneliness when you blame it on someone else.
Y is for younger people that are getting hurt.
I is for sadness inside.
N is for no bullying going on here.
G is for goodness if you leave them alone.

John Kelly (11)
St Joseph's Primary School, Dunloy

Angry

A ngry I hate.
N o way, I do not want to be angry.
G rrr, I hate being angry and cross.
R evenge on someone who makes me angry.
Y es, I will try not to be angry anymore.

John Smyth (10)
St Joseph's Primary School, Dunloy

I Felt Guilt When

I felt guilt when
I broke my brother's model.
I felt guilt when
I hurt my friends.
I felt guilt when
I sprayed my dad's shaving cream.
I felt guilt when
I played a prank on my friends.

Christopher Logan (11)
St Joseph's Primary School, Dunloy

Homework

Homework, oh homework
I dislike it so much
If I ever forget it
The teacher makes a fuss.
He says, 'No excuses Joseph!'
I get annoyed with all the work we have to do
Whoever invented it they must be mad.

Joseph McAllister (11)
St Joseph's Primary School, Dunloy

My First Cat

My first cat was black and white
It would never get itself in a fight,
Although sometimes into a rage
And he climbed into his cage.
But after all the fun,
His time on Earth was done.

Ciaran McCamphill (10)
St Joseph's Primary School, Dunloy

Turn Over The Page

I'm walking out the door
I feel I should have studied more,
I'm sitting at my desk
Ready to start the test!

My stomach is churning,
My brain is burning,
My legs are shaking,
My heart is breaking.

I'm feeling a-fluster,
My mind's all a cluster,
This is hell
I hope I do well.

'Turn over the page and . . . begin.'

Shannon Mullan (11)
St Joseph's Primary School, Dunloy

Soccer

S is for soccer, oh what a game.
O is for outrageous decisions by the referee.
C is for counter attacks up and down the right and left wings.
C is for countries and clubs we all support.
E is for effort and commitment put into training and games.
R is for relief going through the crowd after the match.

Nicky McKeague (11)
St Joseph's Primary School, Dunloy

Web-Slinger

I wake up with a start, I look above my head,
I see that little spider crawling onto my bed.
I feel it on my foot, it's crawling up my leg,
I think that little spider is on my little head.

James McFall (9)
St Joseph's Primary School, Dunloy

My Boxer Dog

My boxer dog is big and tough
And when I play with her she's really rough.
She is black as night, her eyes are bright,
I really love my boxer dog.

She lives in a dog house in my backyard,
I feel she is a really tough guard.
She's fast as light and loves to bite,
That's why I love my boxer dog.

Kieran Hughes (10)
St Joseph's Primary School, Dunloy

The Fierce Arachnid

Watch out everyone,
Watch out for the . . .
Spider.

He's sure to strike.
Warn the queen bee.
He could be anywhere,
So watch out, *aaaaaaah . . . !*

Joseph Dowds (9)
St Joseph's Primary School, Dunloy

Fear

I don't like you,
You make me feel scared,
But then again you can stop us
From jumping off a cliff.
You stop us from cutting off our fingers,
You stop us from putting a pencil in our eyes,
But I still don't like you.
Unfortunately, I have to stick with you.

Christy Drain (10)
St Joseph's Primary School, Dunloy

The Butterfly

Beautiful butterfly stood on a tree,
You are a butterfly who says, '1, 2, 3.'
The butterfly can fly really, really fast,
The butterfly's wings are really, really class.
Elegant butterfly,
Rose is its name,
Fly away to the rose bush . . . in shame.
Lovely pattern,
Yellow and green.

Rebecca Lewis (9)
St Joseph's Primary School, Dunloy

Oh How I Wish I Was The Queen

Oh how I wish I was the queen,
I could make myself look glamorous,
Or make myself look cross.
My favourite food would be ice cream with strawberry sauce.
But I never will be royal,
I will always be playing in the soil
And getting very, very dirty.

Adara McKendry (11)
St Joseph's Primary School, Dunloy

Embarrassed

I am a musical girl,
But when I get on stage,
I feel I'm going to hurl.
I play the wrong note,
They think it's quite a joke,
I feel . . . *embarrassed!*

Caitriona Boyle (11)
St Joseph's Primary School, Dunloy

The Leader

Six-legged, slender and sly,
Queen of all the ants.
She can fly, but they can't.
What is she . . . ?
The queen ant!

Sorcha Doherty (9)
St Joseph's Primary School, Dunloy

The Mollusc

Moist mollusc,
Juicy and fat,
Camouflaged bug.
What am I?
Of course . . . I am a slug!

Niamh McAuley (10)
St Joseph's Primary School, Dunloy

Spiders

Spiders are creepy-crawly.
They scare people at night.
They never come back again until it is night.
They make people run away, giving them a great fright.

James Kearns (9)
St Joseph's Primary School, Dunloy

The Caterpillar

Creepy-crawly caterpillar
Climbing up the wall
Looking for a juicy leaf,
I hope he doesn't fall.

Sean Hurl (10)
St Joseph's Primary School, Dunloy

Butterfly

B utterflies are fun
U nless you hurt them, of course.
T urning and twisting,
T otally adorable,
E xtremely colourful.
R ound the garden they fly,
F lipping and flapping their wings.
L ovable insects, of course,
Y ou would know one if you saw it.

Stephanie McKendry (10)
St Joseph's Primary School, Dunloy

Caring

C is to be taking good care of somebody.
A is for always being responsible.
R is for ringing to offer some help.
I is for injury and I would get help.
N is never being bad.
G is for being good.

Keiran O'Loan (11)
St Joseph's Primary School, Dunloy

Feeling Sad

My face is swelling,
My eyes are watery,
I'm feeling really sad.
I'm about to cry,
But I try to hold it in.
I'm feeling really sad.

Joanne Traynor (10)
St Joseph's Primary School, Dunloy

Nervous

I was nervous when I did my exam,
So everyone told me to be calm.
I had a plan,
Which was to study when I can,
And that is why I think
I've done well in my exam.

Lauren Elliott (10)
St Joseph's Primary School, Dunloy

Anger

My anger is uncontrollable,
It gets me into trouble,
And that is why when I get angry,
My blood begins to bubble.

My anger is uncontrollable,
It makes my whole brain burn,
And at the end it all depends
On what happens next turn.

Patrick Martin (11)
St Joseph's Primary School, Dunloy

Bee

Some people think it's just a pest.
I like it that much,
I think it's just the best.

Whizzing about in the air
As if without a care,
So protective of his family.
That's my story of the *bee*.

Paul Cochrane (10)
St Joseph's Primary School, Dunloy

Curious, Colourful Crabs

Curious, colourful crab,
I watch you as you crawl,
Although you
Can only go sideways.
You have a very painful snip,
I'm sure I wouldn't want
A snip from you . . .
Ouch!

John O'Neill (9)
St Joseph's Primary School, Dunloy

Feeling Down

H urt is when people talk about me behind my back.
U sually if clothes can't fit, I feel sad and I cry.
R eturn to my bedroom sad and worried, why is it me?
T rying to lose weight, walking and running,
but I don't lose any at all, worried and sad.

James McGowan (10)
St Joseph's Primary School, Dunloy

Slow Sophie Snail

S he is a slow and slimy little snail,
N ot always that friendly,
A lot of snails hate to see her come
I t makes them all run
L onely, however, this doesn't seem to stop little Sophie,
as she still has lots of fun.

Gemma Weir (10)
St Joseph's Primary School, Dunloy

Bees

Bees, bees, buzzy bees,
Eating honey, very funny,
Every day's no holiday
Because it's work, not play.
Bees, bees, busy, buzzy bees.

Caoimhe McCullagh (10)
St Joseph's Primary School, Dunloy

In The Morning

In the morning
It's always a rush,
Running around,
'Get the hairbrush.'

In the house there's
Always a worry,
Having no time
So we have to hurry.

Out of the house,
Through the gate,
'Come on,' said Mum,
'We're going to be late!'

Lock the door
And in the car,
'It won't start, we'll have to walk,
Come on, it's not too far.'

Turn the corner,
Past the gate,
At school at last,
Oh no, I'm late.

Amy McCorry (10)
St Joseph's Primary School, Crumlin

I Begged

I begged my mum
To get a dog.
I asked her every day.
I asked her on holiday.
I asked her every week.

Every time I asked,
It was always the same.
And every day
I looked through the shop window
I saw all the little puppies barking.

I begged and begged.
Oh, what I would give
To have a little puppy
Of my own.

Anne McAllister (9)
St Joseph's Primary School, Crumlin

My Mum

She has beautiful long, black hair.
When she smiles, it makes me happy,
And when I look at her in the photo frame,
I feel sad and miss her a lot.

I think about her every day.
Her Sunday dinners are the best.
Her hugs and kisses beat the rest.
I love her the best.

Kevin McCabe (10)
St Joseph's Primary School, Crumlin

My Mum Is Like A Flower

I love my mum,
She makes me soup when I'm sick,
She tucks me into bed at night,
She listens to me read.
She always makes me laugh,
She always has time to listen to me.
She is like a blooming flower
That will never die away.

Kerry Woulfe (10)
St Joseph's Primary School, Crumlin

Acting

I've wanted to act all my life,
Well, since I saw the movie, 'A Child's Work Life'.

I asked my mum to take me to drama school,
We tried acting like swans, I was more like a bull.

It didn't work out, ah well,
I'll just have to ring a different bell.

Lauren Dwyer (9)
St Joseph's Primary School, Crumlin

First Day Back

First day back,
Homework, I bet.
Work all day, rules to obey,
Sit up straight, don't talk back,
Three o'clock I said, 'Bye, I'm not coming back.'

Nicole Donaghy (9)
St Joseph's Primary School, Crumlin

My Wish

Oh to have a pussy cat,
One that will love and care for me,
One that will be friendly,
To me, my mum and family.

On Christmas Day,
I wish for a pussy cat.
His name will be Timothy.

Christmas Day has arrived,
A box, some toys, what a surprise.
I look in the box and what do I see,
But little pussy, Timothy.

Lucy Smart (10)
St Joseph's Primary School, Crumlin

On The Beach

On the beach there are lots of beautiful things.
On the beach, children play in the sand.
On the beach, birds fly about with flapping wings.
On the beach, toddler swimmers wear rubber bands.

On the beach it is sunny and hot.
On the beach there are sea creatures and crabs.
On the beach there is seaweed and rocks,
But the most beautiful thing I see on the beach
Is the sunset over the sea.

Tom Barnes (10)
St Joseph's Primary School, Crumlin

Work

Work, work, it's always the same,
Maths and English they have no game.

Some people like it,
Most people don't.

Work, work, I really hate it,
I even hate whoever made it.

I wish I could just tear it up,
But I can't because I'm not allowed.

A teacher's favourite word is work,
But they're like trolls who seek and lurk.

Teachers know you don't like work,
But in the end it's all you need.

Connor McCreanor (10)
St Joseph's Primary School, Crumlin

Forced Rhymes

During the day
In the middle of May,
It was my sister's birthday.
We went to buy her some clay,
Then we had a traffic delay.

We went home
And we got her a phone,
And that was the end of the day.

Aoife McKavanagh (9)
St Joseph's Primary School, Crumlin

Thinking

What is my poem going to be about?

Could it be about animals?
Could it be about colours?
Could it be about nature,
Or even art?

Could it be about people?
Could it be about books?
Could it be about school,
Or even trees?

Could it be about fruit?
Could it be about jobs?
Could it be about me?
Could it be about everything or anything?

Nadine McGarry (10)
St Joseph's Primary School, Crumlin

Fire, Fire!

Fire, fire swoops and crashes!
Fire, fire swirls and thrashes!

Fire, fire, why are you here?
Fire, fire, why do I fear?

Fire, fire, stay away.
Fire, fire, what do you say?

Fire, fire swoops and crashes!
Fire, fire swirls and thrashes!

Jarlath Mulhern (10)
St Joseph's Primary School, Crumlin

Funky Flo

I once met a cool creature
Who had many a strange feature.
Wings as soft as a teddy,
Eyes as gold as stars,
Fur as warm as the sun,
Ears as sharp as daggers,
A nose as flat as a sheet,
Lips as green as a grasshopper,
Skin as multicoloured as a pot of markers,
Horns as odd as an alien,
Voice as funky as a chick,
Hair as soft as a kitten,
A belt as shiny as the moon,
Teeth as white as snow,
And a heart as warm as Egypt.

Kate Lagan (8)
St Mary's Primary School, Greenlough

Bruce

I once met an odd creature,
Who had many a strange feature.
Feet as hairy as wolves',
Hair as sharp as knives,
Wings as big as a house,
Tail as fluffy as a kitten,
Ears as scaly as a fish,
His neck was as long as a snake,
His teeth as hard as rocks,
And his heart was as warm
As freshly-baked bread.

Paul Carey (9)
St Mary's Primary School, Greenlough

Jonathan's Hands

I like my hands.
My hands can fold paper to make ships.
They can hold a pen or be bold,
they also pick up new things
and throw away old.
At a pantomime they can clap
or slap people on the back.
They lift up bricks to make a wall.
My hands nip, but cannot flip,
they can discover and touch
wonderful, brand new things.
They can open doors to
brand new places,
and tie my shoelaces,
and they can squeeze the juice
into the glass . . .

Jonathan McAteer (8)
St Mary's Primary School, Greenlough

Aidan's Hands

My hands are excellent,
They flick nuts all over the place,
And they tie my shoelaces
In all sorts of new places.
They help me catch a ball
Before I go to the mall.
They find a pip
And help me get
A good grip.
Sometimes they can be
As good as gold,
And sometimes they can be bold.

Aidan McErlean (8)
St Mary's Primary School, Greenlough

Aimee's Feet

I like my feet.
They can dance
And they can prance.
My feet can run
And they can be lots of fun.
My feet can help me swim,
But they can't say, 'Hello,'
To my friend, Tim.
They can stamp,
But they can't turn on a lamp.
They can also walk,
But they can never talk.
They tiptoe to the tiny turtles,
Sometimes they skip
Through the hurdles.
They can be as
Brown as bark,
But mostly they are
As white as snow.
They always take me
Where I need to go . . .

Aimee Cassidy (9)
St Mary's Primary School, Greenlough

Travelling

Travelling on stilts can be great,
Proud to be so tall.
Peering down at the people I hate,
Walking on my way home.

Travelling on roller coasters can be a blast,
Sick of twisting around.
Mouths open as we go frighteningly fast,
As we stop, I hit my face.

Roisin McCloskey (9)
St Mary's Primary School, Greenlough

Star Shapes

A star is a diamond
in the ever-changing sky,
it's a dove's wing
gracefully fluttering by.

A star is a pair of sandals
with a shiny buckle,
it's a lava lamp
on a dark wall.

A star is a pattern
on night's beautiful face,
it's a torch
lighting up angels' dresses, made of lace.

A star is a light
shining everywhere,
it's a white animal
never a grumpy bear.

Orla McErlean (7)
St Mary's Primary School, Greenlough

Niall's Mouth

I like my mouth.
My mouth can bite,
But it cannot fly a kite.
Sometimes my mouth
Helps me slurp when I drink.
When I whisper, it's as gentle as a breeze.
It can roar like a tiger on the prowl.
My mouth can scream
When I want ice cream.
Sometimes my mouth
Can chew very hard things.

Niall Loughlin (9)
St Mary's Primary School, Greenlough

Friendship

We like to run races,
And make funny faces.
We like to act cool,
With a dip in the pool.

He wears a top from Glen,
It annoys Greenlough men.
He's got some blond hair,
Stripy jeans he'll wear.

He makes me laugh when I'm sad,
I'm telling you he's never bad.
When his team loses, he's not unhappy,
When he's tired, he can be snappy.

Michael Og Lagan (10)
St Mary's Primary School, Greenlough

Friendship

A jump into the pool,
And keep ourselves cool.
We like throwing stones,
And pretending we are looking for dinosaur bones.

He has short black hair,
And he roars like a bear.
His eyes are shiny blue,
And he wears a size 7 shoe.

When he scores a goal it makes him excited,
And when he is at my house he is delighted.
School makes him sad.
When I stay at his house for the weekend he is glad.

Christopher McPeake (9)
St Mary's Primary School, Greenlough

Tower

When I live in my tower,
I shall keep in my tower
Two twisted thieves,
Three terrible tadpoles,
Four frozen fish,
Five fizzy floors,
Six singing seals,
Seven shiny sheep,
Eight Easter eggs,
Nine nasty newts,
Ten tasty treats,
One wonderful wizard,
That's what I'll have in my tower.

Catherine Morren (9)
St Mary's Primary School, Greenlough

Palace

When I live in my palace,
I shall keep in my palace,
Two tiny turtles,
Three tremendous tables,
Four famous faces,
Five fierce fairies,
Six scary skeletons,
Seven sleepy slaves,
Eight extra elephants,
Nine naughty neighbours,
Ten tiptoeing toddlers and
One orange organiser,
That's what I'll have in my palace.

Emma Mooney (8)
St Mary's Primary School, Greenlough

Mansion

When I live in my mansion,
I shall keep in my mansion,
Two terrible televisions,
Three tiny toys,
Four fast fish,
Five fat fingers,
Six singing sea lions,
Seven stinging scorpions,
Eight enormous elephants,
Nine naughty newts,
Ten tiny tractors
And one wicked witch,
That's what I'll have in my mansion.

Ryan McGoldrick (9)
St Mary's Primary School, Greenlough

Castle

When I live in a castle,
I shall keep in my castle,
Two terrible telephones,
Three tiny toilets,
Four fancy flowers,
Five fiery frogs,
Six slimy seagulls,
Seven stinky scorpions.
Eight Easter eggs,
Nine tasty noodles,
Ten tangled taps
And one wonderful wagon,
That's what I'll have in my castle.

Aimee Bedell (9)
St Mary's Primary School, Greenlough

Star Shapes

A star is a diamond
twinkling up above.
It's a white rabbit
tingling with love.

A star is a daisy,
so very white.
It's a lava lamp
lighting up so bright.

A star is a butterfly,
so colourful and small.
It's a raindrop
that will never fall.

Elish Madden (8)
St Mary's Primary School, Greenlough

Bungalow

When I live in a bungalow,
I shall keep in my bungalow,
Two talking toads,
Three tipping toes,
Four flipping frogs,
Five flying funfairs,
Six slithering snakes,
Seven sick students,
Eight Eddy elephants,
Ten tricky tractors
And one wobbly waiter,
That's what I'll have in my bungalow.

Caolan Diamond (8)
St Mary's Primary School, Greenlough

Star Shape

A star is a swan
swimming on moon's lake.
It's a little white creature
scurrying on a snowflake.

A star is a firework
shooting up on high.
It's a colourful object
banging in the bright sky.

A star is a gold button
shining so bright.
It's a little gold spark
glowing so bright.

A star is a raindrop
falling down night's face.
It's a snowflake
filling every little space.

Fionn Hamill (8)
St Mary's Primary School, Greenlough

The Sea

The sea can tear,
The sea can splash,
The sea is unfair,
Like cars going to crash.

The sea can be gentle,
The sea can be kind,
The sea can be smooth,
Like something good to find.

Sarah McCann (8)
St Mary's Primary School, Greenlough

Star Shape

A star is a firework
exploding in the sky,
it's a snowflake
waving bye-bye.

A star is a diamond,
twinkling in the night,
it's a torch
giving everyone light.

A star is an angel
looking down,
it's my mum
in her night-gown.

Claire McErlain (8)
St Mary's Primary School, Greenlough

I Like

I like the taste of soup
sliding down my tongue.

I like the smell of flowers
gliding up my nose.

I like the feel of donkeys
tickling my face.

I like the sound of chapel bells
singing in my ears.

I like the sight of kittens
purring all day long.

Aine McErlean (8)
St Mary's Primary School, Greenlough

Star Shapes

A star is a sparkling diamond
on the edge of a ring.
It's a golden bird
starting to sing.

A star is a glittering fish
swimming in a dish.
It's a shining ring
making a wish.

A star is a golden pattern
like a beautiful shining sun.
It's an ocean where you have
lots of fun.

Michaela Lynn (7)
St Mary's Primary School, Greenlough

I Like . . .

I like the taste of jelly
sliding on my tongue.

I like the smell of bacon
swirling up my nose.

I like the feel of snowflakes
tickling on my face.

I like the sound of hailstones
crashing in my ears.

I like the sight of stars
twinkling in the sky.

Caoimhe McNally (8)
St Mary's Primary School, Greenlough

Friendship

We go to the shops
And try on different tops,
We gather up grass,
We serve together at mass.

She's quite tall,
But I am very small.
Her eyes are blue,
Her hair is brown too.

Seeing dogs make her delighted,
Camogie makes her excited.
She's very funny
And makes my life very sunny.

Pauline Madden (10)
St Mary's Primary School, Greenlough

My Friend

We have fun in any sort of way,
We go to each other's houses and stay.
We play and jump and sing,
She lets me borrow her silver ring.

She has green eyes
And never tells lies.
A silver ring she will always wear
And she has long, curly brown-blonde hair.

When I'm sad
She makes me glad,
She makes me snigger,
She is generous, you figure?

Shannon Rafferty (9)
St Mary's Primary School, Greenlough

Friendship

We laugh, we run, we sing and play,
That's what we do every day.
We talk and talk all day long,
We love to sing our favourite song.

She wears her glasses, always glittering,
Her eyelashes are always flickering.
She has long blonde wavy hair,
Her big blue eyes always glare.

She makes me feel special in a funny kind of way,
Excites me nearly every day.
Clever at making me feel good,
When I'm in a bad mood.

Clare Doherty (10)
St Mary's Primary School, Greenlough

My Friend

We both like to climb trees,
And catch bumblebees.
We go for a long walk,
Then we have a talk.

He has short black hair,
On his T-shirt is a bear.
He has shiny brown eyes
And he doesn't like wearing ties.

I delight him with a present,
His nature is pleasant.
When I upset him he is sad,
He is rarely mad.

James Duffin (10)
St Mary's Primary School, Greenlough

Friendship

It's fun when we go to the pool,
Especially the deep end, the small one's not as cool.
Me and you together as friends,
When we play football, you win in the end.

You always wear a Derry shirt,
You go out clean and come in covered in dirt.
Your eyes are sparkly blue,
Your hair sticks up like glue.

Sweets make him glad,
Girls' stuff makes him mad.
Football makes him act crazy,
Only sometimes, he is lazy.

Emma McErlain (9)
St Mary's Primary School, Greenlough

Riding On A Horse

Riding on a horse can be fun,
Relaxed as I'm trotting on a path of tar.
Walking my horse in the hot sizzling sun,
In Peatlands Park in Armagh.

Riding on a horse can be fun
Nervous as I get on.
Prancing through the fields as other horses run,
Coming to a stop at the end.

Gráinne Maguire (9)
St Mary's Primary School, Greenlough

Friendship

We make a prank call,
We play basketball.
Race cars down a tube,
We spend hours together on the Game Cube.

He's thin
Has very pale skin,
Arsenal shirt, he loves to wear,
He has short brown hair.

Crisps make him delighted,
Arsenal scoring makes him excited.
He never makes me sad,
I never make him mad.

Robert Kelly (10)
St Mary's Primary School, Greenlough

Friendship

We each have a part to play,
Keeping the other happy, each day.
We talk about our fears,
We share all our tears.

Her hair is blonde,
It's layered and quite long.
Her cheeks are as red as a rose,
She's such a pose.

She's generous to me as well,
Makes me laugh with the stories she tells,
I frighten her when I do silly things,
Gets very mad when I begin to sing.

Colleen McErlean (10)
St Mary's Primary School, Greenlough

Friendship

We walk to the shop,
We share fizzy pop.
We're always running races
And eating liquorice laces.

She's got ginger hair,
Her favourite T-shirt says, 'Very Rare'.
She is so thin
And she's got fair skin.

Dogs give her a fright,
But cats give her a spark of light.
Her sister makes her mad
When we argue she's sad.

Shauna Quinn (10)
St Mary's Primary School, Greenlough

Seanin's Mouth

My mouth can chat on the phone,
But it can't pay a car loan.
It drooled when I was young,
And carried air into my lung.
Sometimes it hides my teeth,
But only when I'm nervous.
When I lick it,
It sparkles like fairies' wings.
My marvellous mouth
Is full of wonder,
And can sing day and night . . .

Seanin Marron (9)
St Mary's Primary School, Greenlough

I Like . . .

I like the taste of crisps
tingling on my tongue.

I like the smell of potatoes
swaying up my nose.

I like the feel of rain
dripping on my face.

I like the sound of bells
ringing in my ears.

I like the sight of children
working in the classroom.

Liza Marie Duffin (8)
St Mary's Primary School, Greenlough

Images In Words

Stars glittering like shining silver moons
Clouds floating like aeroplanes
Waves crashing like an earthquake
The wind blowing like windy stars
Mist creeping like a ghost
The moon shining like a lighthouse
A river twisting like a twisting ear
A volcano smoking like fire, smoking.

Orlagh McAfee (8)
St Patrick's & St Brigid's School, Ballycastle

Untitled

Dashing to get my lunch box,
I am hungry, it's very nice and good.
My favourite food is spaghetti Bolognese and chips.
The food I don't like is rice.

Ronan Blaney (8)
St Patrick's & St Brigid's School, Ballycastle

Images With Words

A forest like a big wild jungle that smells like
nature all around.

Stars glittering like the groovy glitter we girls
can wear on our faces.

Babies crying like a packet of baby potatoes trying
to get attention, so we will take them out.

A vacuum cleaner like a house eater or sucker,
trying to suck and eat the house, making our
lives a misery.

Tadpoles like small worms wiggling in the water
that turn into half frog and half worm.

A volcano like a person, about to blow up and
flutter around the room, like a balloon when you
let the air out.

Spaghetti like slimy, skinny slugs instead of fat ones
trying to slide off my plate.

Mairead McHenry (9)
St Patrick's & St Brigid's School, Ballycastle

Images With Words

Stars glittering like the Queen's gems,
A river twisting like vines.
The wind blowing like a fan cooling me down,
Mist creeping like a spider making its web.
A worm wriggling like water falling,
Clouds floating like a blimp in the sky.
A volcano smoking like a cigarette,
The moon shining like a chandelier.
The waves crashing like a vase falling.

Jenny McHenry (8)
St Patrick's & St Brigid's School, Ballycastle

Untitled

The wind blowing like a big bad wolf
blowing on the pigs' houses.
Mist creeping like wanted crooks
robbing a house.
A volcano smoking like a teenager
who made a bad choice.
Waves crashing like a broken car
in an accident.
A river twisting like a roller coaster
twisting round and round.
Stars glittering like jewels
sparkling in the sky.
Trees growing like children
each year.

Hugh Neill (9)
St Patrick's & St Brigid's School, Ballycastle

Untitled

Mist creeping like spiders crawling
in the bath,

Waves crashing like a bomb
in the war.

Clouds floating like a swallow
in the breeze.

A river twisting like a massive
lighthouse.

The wind blowing like a lion
when it roars.

A worm wriggling like a viper
on the ground.

Shane Devlin (8)
St Patrick's & St Brigid's School, Ballycastle

Images And Words

Stars glittering like diamonds shimmering,
reflecting the sun.

A river twisting like a fish
swimming in the sea.

Clouds floating like a whipped cream and orange sunset,
could be an apple pie, just hovering above.

The wind blowing like a fan blowing
the loveliest breeze around the room.

Mist creeping like a caterpillar trying
to make its way through the garden.

A worm wriggling like some spaghetti
moving all around my plate.

Waves crashing like a thunderbolt
absolutely smashing the ground.

A volcano smoking like a bonfire, bright
burning colours, red, yellow and orange.

The moon shining like the stars
twinkling in the dark night's sky.

Bronagh McCaughan (8)
St Patrick's & St Brigid's School, Ballycastle

White Narnia

White looks like snow,
It sounds like seashells getting dropped on the beach,
White smells salty, like the sea.
It feels soft as a polar bear's fur,
White tastes like ice cream.

The White Witch rules Narnia,
And makes it winter, but never Christmas!
The white snow falls down onto the ground,
Falling, falling endlessly.

Shannon Mullan (7)
St Patrick's & St Brigid's School, Ballycastle

Images With Word

A river twisting like a big tornado
which comes from the sky,

A volcano smoking like a fire
on a cold night which burns brightly.

The moon shining like a sun on a
hot summer's day, by the beach.

Clouds floating like candyfloss
from Heaven above.

Stars glittering like a light
in the middle of the night.

Ciarrai Guihan (8)
St Patrick's & St Brigid's School, Ballycastle

I Asked The Girl Who Cannot See

I asked the girl who cannot see,
'What is colour like for you?'
'Green is like a mint ice cream,
Pink is a rose we have to smell.
White is snow falling from the sky,
Red is the smell of roses,
Yellow is like the sun heating you.'

Alvin Baby (8)
St Patrick's & St Brigid's School, Ballycastle

I Asked The Girl Who Cannot See

I ask the little girl who cannot see,
'What is colour like for you?'
'Green is like feeling grass,
Red is like the smell of roses.
Yellow is like the sun's heat you.'

Lisa Warn (7)
St Patrick's & St Brigid's School, Ballycastle

Untitled

The wind blowing like Superman
blowing over a fire with his freezing breath.

A river twisting like party streamers
at a birthday party.

Mist creeping like a zombie coming
to capture and eat you.

Stars glittering like pixie dust
falling from the sky.

The moon shining like gold you've just found
in a treasure chest.

Waves crashing like a machine through
a brick wall.

A volcano smoking like a cigarette
in the distance.

Clouds floating like a human being
in a swimming pool.

Worms wriggling like spaghetti
all over your plate.

Darren McGuigan (8)
St Patrick's & St Brigid's School, Ballycastle

I Asked The Little Girl Who Cannot See

I asked the little girl who cannot see,
'What is colour like for you?'

'Blue is like the roaring sea, the waves
rolling onto the land,
Green is like mint ice cream, soft, cold
and minty to eat.
Yellow is like the very hot sun that shines
on a summer's day.
Red is a Liverpool flag swaying in the breeze.'

Jimmy McKiernan (8)
St Patrick's & St Brigid's School, Ballycastle

I Asked The Little Girl Who Cannot See

I asked the little girl who cannot see,
'What is colour like for you?'

'Yellow is like the smell of a daffodil,
Pink is like the smell of a flower.
Blue is for the beautiful sky,
Red is for the red flaming fire.
Green is for the green grass.'

Elora-danan Kinney (8)
St Patrick's & St Brigid's School, Ballycastle

I Asked The Little Girl Who Cannot See

I asked the little girl who cannot see,
'What is colour like for you?'

'Pink is like the feel of soft roses,
Green is like hard cabbage.
Blue is like cold ice cream,
Yellow is like a shining sun.
White is like a big cold snowman,
Brown is like a stick.'

Sinéad Brown (8)
St Patrick's & St Brigid's School, Ballycastle

I Asked The Little Girl Who Cannot See

I asked the little girl who cannot see,
'What is colour like for you?'

'Green is like tasty peas,
Orange is like a tasty orange.
Brown is like tasty chocolate cake.
Red is like a nice-smelling rose,
Yellow is like the sun.'

Catherine Curran (8)
St Patrick's & St Brigid's School, Ballycastle

I Asked The Little Girl Who Cannot See

I asked the little girl who cannot see,
'What is colour like for you?'

'Blue is like waves splashing in the sea,
Green is like the grass on the ground.
Red is the flaming fire,
Silver is shining metal.
Brown is like a chocolate milkshake rolling
over your tongue.
Yellow is like the sun shining.'

Conor Spence (8)
St Patrick's & St Brigid's School, Ballycastle

I Asked The Little Girl Who Cannot See

I asked the little girl who cannot see,
'What is colour like for you?'
'Red is like an Arsenal top when you pull it on and off.
Brown tastes like Diet Pepsi, bouncing on my tongue.
I can hear the blue sea bashing against the shore,
I can hear the crowd shouting, 'Arsenal!''

Sean Maxwell (8)
St Patrick's & St Brigid's School, Ballycastle

I Asked The Little Girl Who Cannot See

I asked the little girl who cannot see,
'What is colour like?'
'Why red,' said she, 'it's like the smell of roses.
Dark blue is the smell of fish.
Pink is a kind of a top.
Light blue is the splashing of a waterfall and
Black and white is the softness of a cat's fur.'

Enya Kate De Wolf (8)
St Patrick's & St Brigid's School, Ballycastle

I Asked The Little Girl Who Cannot See

I asked the little girl who cannot see,
'What is colour like for you?'
She said to me . . .
'Brown is like a chocolate milkshake rolling
over your tongue.
Orange is like the sun making sweat
drop down your face.
Green is for leaves, swaying in the breeze.
Red is for a really *hot* flaming fire,
Blue is for a nice running waterfall.'

Cathal Connor (8)
St Patrick's & St Brigid's School, Ballycastle

The Little Girl Who Could Not See

I asked the little girl who could not see,
'What is colour like for you?'
She replied, 'Why green is a cabbage,
it's so crunchy on my teeth.
Well white is crunchy snow, which is cold
and crispy all over the ground.
Pink is a salmon, all fishy and smelly.
I really like fish in my belly.
And red is roses bright and nice.'

Aoife Walsh (8)
St Patrick's & St Brigid's School, Ballycastle

I Asked The Little Girl Who Cannot See

I asked the little girl who cannot see,
'What is colour like for you?'

'Green is the grass that you run and step on,
Green is when the leaves sway in the breeze.
Green is when you eat cabbage for your dinner.'

Ronan McAfee (8)
St Patrick's & St Brigid's School, Ballycastle

I Asked The Little Girl Who Cannot See

'What is colour for you?'
'Red is like the smell of a rose,
Blue is like swimming in the sea.
White is like bouncing a ball,
Green is like playing in the grass.
Orange is my favourite colour,
Yellow is like a daffodil.
Pink is like a flower,
Black is like the night,
Brown is like a door.'

Emma Smylie (8)
St Patrick's & St Brigid's School, Ballycastle

I Asked The Girl Who Could Not See

I asked the girl who could not see,
'What is colour like for you?'

'Blue is like water dripping out of a tap,
Red is like delicious strawberries you eat.
White is like snowflakes falling on my hand,
Yellow is like the heat of a hot day.
Orange is like the oranges we eat.
Black is like a black wheelchair.'

Riona McCambridge (7)
St Patrick's & St Brigid's School, Ballycastle

I Asked The Little Girl Who Cannot See

I asked the little girl who cannot see,
'What is colour like for you?'
'Red is the colour of the sun blazing
like fire.
Brown is the colour of chocolate,
tasty and sweet.'

Daniel Morgan (8)
St Patrick's & St Brigid's School, Ballycastle

I Asked The Little Girl Who Could Not See

I asked the little girl who could not see,
'What is colour like for you?'
'Orange is like something soft and warm,
Black is a thundercloud.
Red is like a single red rose,
Blue is like a running tap.
Pink is like a packet of bubblegum.
Yellow is like the sun in your eyes,
Brown is like a chocolate milkshake.
White is like winter snow.'

Fionnula Mooney (8)
St Patrick's & St Brigid's School, Ballycastle

Animals

A is for ants eating some fruit
N is for a naughty, nocturnal owl
I is for a hippy, hoppy inset
M is for a mad, bad monkey
A is for a swampy, smelly alligator
L is for lambs with some green grass
S is for a slithery, slippery snake.

Neill Ronald Duncan (9)
St Patrick's & St Brigid's School, Ballycastle

Animals

A is for alligator, a sharp-toothed alligator.
N is for nocturnal, a nocturnal owl.
I is for insect, an interesting insect.
M is for monkey, a really mad monkey.
A is for ant, a little tiny ant.
L is for ladybird, a little dotty ladybird.
S is for snake, a slithery, slimy snake.

Caoimhe Hyland (9)
St Patrick's & St Brigid's School, Ballycastle

The Little Girl Who Cannot See

I asked the little girl who cannot see,
'What is colour like for you?'
'Black is a dream in a cave.
Green is grass crunching away,
Green is leaves swaying, side to side.
Green is ice cream, mint and cold.
Red is a lovely rose that smells so good.
Brown is like a chocolate milkshake
Rolling over your tongue.
Brown is like a roaring grizzly bear,
Green is a cabbage, crunching on my teeth.'

Erin McBride (8)
St Patrick's & St Brigid's School, Ballycastle

Animals

A is for ants crawling in the forest
N is for nocturnal owls,
I is for insects crawling in the ground.
M is for monkeys, swinging in the trees.
A is for alligators swimming in the river.
L is for lions looking after their cubs,
S is for snakes, slithering on the ground.

Abbie McNeill (9)
St Patrick's & St Brigid's School, Ballycastle

Animals

A ntelopes, nearly as fast as cheetahs,
N octurnal animals come out at night,
I love every single animal,
M ammals, animals, they give their babies milk,
A nt hills, full of busy ants,
L adybirds, tiny flying insects,
S nakes, slithering along jungle floors.

Alice Mee (9)
St Patrick's & St Brigid's School, Ballycastle

White Is A Cold Colour

White looks like the snow,
It feels like polar bear fur.
White tastes like a birthday cake,
It sounds like an angel singing.
White smells like daisies.

The Snow Queen is white,
Her dress is blue and white.
She's not very nice,
Her house is made with ice.

Rachel Woodhouse (8)
St Patrick's & St Brigid's School, Ballycastle

White Angel

White looks like a cloud,
It sounds like a gull flying.
White smells like ice cream,
It tastes like candyfloss.
It feels fluffy.

White is like an angel,
Flying in the air.
From Heaven to Earth,
With her wings coming down from Heaven above.

Laura McQuilkin (7)
St Patrick's & St Brigid's School, Ballycastle

Holidays

Holidays are so much fun,
You can run along the beach,
Play and have fun or bury yourself in the sand.
Oh holidays are so much fun,
I can go anywhere,
But I don't care as long as I'm in the sun.

Danielle McMichael (9)
St Patrick's & St Brigid's School, Ballycastle

I Asked The Girl Who Could Not See

I asked the girl who could not see,
'What is colour like for you?'
'Cream is like the skin on my face,
Blue is like the rain on my window.
Orange is like the sun hitting my face.
Yellow is like a slippery banana,
Green is like the trees blowing,
Grey is like the clouds in the sky.
Yellow is like a lion's roar
White is like the snow, melting on my hand.'

Bronagh Clarke (8)
St Patrick's & St Brigid's School, Ballycastle

Friends

F is for friendly
R is for respectable
I is for interesting
E is for explorer
N is for natural
D is for delightful
S is for special friend - just like this one.

Megan Mooney (9)
St Patrick's & St Brigid's School, Ballycastle

Animals

A is for ants,
N is for nice, cuddly dogs,
I is for insects, so creepy,
M is for monkeys,
A is for an alligator,
L is for lovely lambs,
S is for slimy snails.

Shannon Hegarty (9)
St Patrick's & St Brigid's School, Ballycastle

Yellow Is Special

Yellow looks like a beautiful butterfly,
It tastes like golden sweetcorn.
Yellow smells like a lovely sunflower.
It sounds like a lemon being squeezed.
Yellow feels like a duckling's soft feathers,
It is like a morning sunrise.

A girl in a yellow dress is going for a walk,
She's walking on the soft sand.
Her golden hair is streaming behind her,
She's a princess with a golden crown.
But now she's taken by the Egyptians,
She's trapped in the gloomy dungeon
With only a ray of sunlight to keep her company.
Luckily she found a little yellow rabbit.
'Yellow is special,' she said.

Hannah McMullan (7)
St Patrick's & St Brigid's School, Ballycastle

White World

White looks like a gentle seagull,
It sounds quiet like glittering snow, falling.
White smells like white roses swaying.
It feels like a smooth turtle.
White tastes like mint chewing gum.
It's like Santa's beard, soft and fluffy.
Chalky stuff that teachers use to teach
And sweet as the birds chirping in the sunset.
The bird lives with her white eggs,
She keeps them warm with her white feathers.
The pale white moon sparkles on her eggs.
It's a cold sight tonight, a cold breeze blows.
It's giving her a clue; tomorrow will be a white world.

Tamara Mooney (7)
St Patrick's & St Brigid's School, Ballycastle

What Happens In The Seasons

What happens in the seasons
Coming to spring
Fairies all want to sing
The unicorns run
The babies have fun
And that's what happens in spring.

Always in the summer
The Trolls get dumber and dumber
Goblins eat clocks
Dwarves break rocks
And that's what happens in summer.

Sometimes in autumn
In the caves you spot them
They're big, bright and red
With a fire-breathing head
It's a dragon.

Usually in winter
Monsters do more than give you a splinter
They tear off your legs
Poke out your eyes with pegs
And that's the bad thing about winter.

Ruairi Kinney (8)
St Patrick's & St Brigid's School, Ballycastle

Sand And Scarecrows

Yellow looks like most of Egypt's sand dunes,
It tastes like golden butter.
Yellow smells like lemons.
It sounds like a roaring tiger.
Yellow feels like soft fur,
Yellow is like lightning.
Golden hair from a girl.
The scarecrows stand in their golden clothes.
Guarding ripening corn.

Collum McKiernan (7)
St Patrick's & St Brigid's School, Ballycastle

Sunset And Red Roses

Red looks like red roses,
It tastes like juicy apples.
Red sounds like a thump on the ground,
It feels like a soft blanket.
Red smells like a hot bonfire.

There's a girl looking at the sunset
In her bright red lipstick.
She has a glass of red wine her hand.
In the other hand she has a bright red rose.
She smells it before she sips her wine.
The sun sets and the old stars are out.
The girl is in her house lying in her bright red room.

Chloe Kelly (8)
St Patrick's & St Brigid's School, Ballycastle

Red Poem

Red looks like red roses,
It tastes like cherry flavour.
Red sounds like a marching band,
It feels like hot fire.
Red smells like cherries.

The girl in the scarlet dress
Wears bright red lipstick.
She walks through a garden of roses,
Lovely crimson flowers,
She sips a glass of red wine.
Lovely dark apple red,
Red looks like blood.

Coleen Cahill (7)
St Patrick's & St Brigid's School, Ballycastle

Hallowe'en Horrors

H aunted houses
A pple dunking
L eaves rustle
L anterns are carried.
O range pumpkins are carved,
W itches fly.
E vil hunchbacks grin,
E veryone has a laugh.
N uts are used in parties, at night.

Connor Norcott (7)
St Patrick's & St Brigid's School, Ballycastle

I Asked The Girl Who Could Not See

I asked the girl who could not see,
'What is colour like for you?'
'White is the colour of snow melting on my hand,
Blue is like the tap dripping,
Green is like the hedges rustling,
Red is like the warmth of the sun.
Pink is like the taste of a marshmallow.
Yellow is like a soft quilt.
Purple is like a cold winter's night.'

Rory Magee (8)
St Patrick's & St Brigid's School, Ballycastle

I Asked The Girl Who Cannot See

'What is colour like for you?'

'Black is a dream in a cave,
Red is a hot fire.
Gold is like a loving handshake,
Silver is like a piece of metal.
Green is like the trees
Pink is like the smell of roses.
Yellow is like the sun,
Blue is like the sea,
Purple must be like a thunderstorm.'

Ryan McFall (8)
St Patrick's & St Brigid's School, Ballycastle

I Asked The Little Girl Who Could Not See

I asked the little girl who could not see,
'What is colour like for you?'

'Brown is like jagged thorns,
Silver is like shining money in your purse,
Pink is like a soft and beautiful rose.
Red is like a berry you eat,
White is like soft and yummy ice cream.
The yellow sun feels like an egg, boiling in the sky.'

Lindsay Horner (8)
St Patrick's & St Brigid's School, Ballycastle

Royal Red

Red looks like a rose falling from the sky,
It tastes like sweet strawberries.
Red sounds like a marching band,
It feels like a soft red blanket.
Red smells like turf on the fire,
Red smells like beautiful roses.
It's like the shimmering sunset,
It's like touching red blood.
Red is like a princess' dress.
It looks like red rubies on the crown.

Cliodhna Devlin (7)
St Patrick's & St Brigid's School, Ballycastle

Red Bonfire

Red looks like a fox creeping by,
Red tastes like sweet berries.
It sounds like a rock band,
It feels like slimy blood.
Red smells like roast turkey.

I watch the scarlet bonfire on Hallowe'en,
The crimson fireworks brighten my eyes.
I fall and out comes red blood.
We go home to eat red strawberries and red turkey.
I get red juice to sip.

Ronan McCarry (7)
St Patrick's & St Brigid's School, Ballycastle

Creatures And Clouds

White looks like a shell,
It sounds like daisies swaying.
White smells like owl's feathers.
It feels like a penguin.
White tastes like strong mints.

The clouds so high,
As white as can be.
They form pictures of faces,
And they look so far away.

Eoin McAuley (7)
St Patrick's & St Brigid's School, Ballycastle

Golden Yellow

Yellow looks like the sun,
It tastes like custard.
It smells like custard on apple pie,
It sounds like custard being poured,
Yellow feels like a duckling.

We are walking on a sandy desert,
And the sun is shining
Like a darling in the beautiful blue sky.
Now we are walking across the dusty yellow road.

Fiona Lagan (7)
St Patrick's & St Brigid's School, Ballycastle

Red Things

Red looks like terrible danger,
It tastes like a sweet apple.
Red sounds like our hearts beating.
It feels like a hawk's feathers.
Red smells like a beautiful rose,
My heater is red.

My mum has scarlet lipstick,
I have red roses in my garden.
Scarlet looks like my teacher's heart.

Siobhan Donnelly (7)
St Patrick's & St Brigid's School, Ballycastle

Wonder World

Yellow looks like a sunflower,
It tastes like sweet honey.
Yellow smells like a daisy sitting in a field.
It sounds like a duckling quacking,
Yellow feels like sand blowing.

The girl with golden hair
Was looking at bright dandelions.
The yellow sun was shining
And yellow-centred daisies were growing.
She saw a duckling looking for its mother.

Caolan McCaughan (7)
St Patrick's & St Brigid's School, Ballycastle

I Asked The Girl Who Could Not See

'What is colour like for you?'
'Peach,' she said, 'is like the baker's buns.
Pink is like a soft marshmallow,
Brown is a tasty hot dog.
Blue is the wavy pool.
Gold is a metal key.
White is a dog's fur rubbing up against me.
Red is a noisy bus.
Silver is like snow melting in my hands.'

Kaelan Killough (8)
St Patrick's & St Brigid's School, Ballycastle

I Asked The Girl Who Could Not See

I asked the girl who could not see,
'What is the colour like for you?'

'Why orange is like a hot, hot day
and cream is like a creamy yoghurt
on my tongue.
Brown is like the thorns on my hand.
Blue is like the tap that drips.
Green is like the trees blowing.
Pink is like a cherry.
Red is like the ice cream on my lips.
White is like the soap when I wash my hands.'

Una Staunton (8)
St Patrick's & St Brigid's School, Ballycastle

Daisy

I've a puppy called Daisy
She's very friendly.
She's also loyal,
But when she's naughty -
She digs up the garden soil.

She barks at the postman at the gate,
My aunty's dog is one of her doggy mates.
She has lots of energy,
But every puppy has to stop
Now she's fallen on the sofa, in a flop.

Caitilin Gormley (9)
St Patrick's & St Brigid's School, Ballycastle

Pets

Pets are easy to feed,
Easy to handle,
My best friends.
So nice and cuddly,
Oh I love pets.

My favourite pet is a dog.

Dogs, dogs, oh how I love dogs,
They are so good and cuddly,
They never run away.
My dog's name is Holly.

Ruiari McKay (9)
St Patrick's & St Brigid's School, Ballycastle

Feeling Happy

I feel happy when Callum and Patrick play with me.
I feel excited when it's my party.
I feel glad when I get gifts.
I feel cheerful when I am at school.

Jamie Greer (8)
The Diamond Primary School

Winter Is . . .

Winter is . . . playing in the snow and building snowmen,
Winter is . . . making footprints all day long,
Winter is . . . playing and singing inside the nice warm house,
Winter is . . . a nice, big, warm Christmas dinner inside,
Winter is . . . sitting by a nice warm fire.

Rachael Carson (8)
The Diamond Primary School

Feeling Happy

I feel happy when my friends come over.
I feel excited when my mummy buys me sweets.
I feel glad when I get a DVD.
I feel cheerful when it is Saturday, because I go dancing.

Erin Herbison (7)
The Diamond Primary School

Winter Is . . .

Winter is . . . to have a snow fight and make snowmen,
Winter is . . . sleeping in,
Winter is . . . eating lovely turkey dinners,
Winter is . . . seeing my uncle Gerry.
Isn't winter the best time of year?

Matthew Kirk (8)
The Diamond Primary School

Feeling Happy

I feel happy when it is summer,
I feel excited when I go to school,
I feel glad when I try my best,
I feel cheerful when I get something nice.

Ben Millar (8)
The Diamond Primary School

Winter Is . . .

Winter is . . . playing in the snow and making snowmen,
Winter is . . . having Christmas dinner and eating it all,
Winter is . . . having no homework to do in the holidays,
Winter is . . . opening presents on Christmas Day,
Winter is . . . decorating the Christmas tree at night,
Winter is . . . sitting in front of the fire,
Winter is . . . *fun!*

Niall Cavanagh (7)
The Diamond Primary School

School

S is for spellings and tables tests,
C is for comprehension,
H is for history and health education,
O is for opening the doors for the teachers,
O is for Oscar Orange,
L is for lovely work.

Callum Herbison (7)
The Diamond Primary School

Winter Is . . .

Winter is . . . making snow angels,
Winter is . . . Christmas holidays,
Winter is . . . sitting at the fire, eating chocolates,
Winter is . . . eating Christmas dinner,
Winter is . . . going to bed early and getting up to see my presents,
Winter is . . . freezing!

Patrick Herbison (7)
The Diamond Primary School

Pussycat, Pussycat

(Inspired by 'Pussycat, Pussycat')

'Pussycat, Pussycat,
Where have you been?'
'I've been to Cullybackey -
A lot to be seen.'
'Pussycat, Pussycat,
What did you there?'
'I went to the hairdressers
And got a perm in my hair!'

Rachael Thompson (10) & Mandy Holmes (11)
The Diamond Primary School

Feeling Happy

I feel happy when I'm going to my friend's house.
I feel excited when Friday comes.
I feel glad when I go to the park.
I feel cheerful when I sing a song.
I feel happy all day long.

Jessica Gibson (8)
The Diamond Primary School

Feeling Happy

I feel happy when I play outside.
I feel excited when Friday comes.
I feel glad when I am 'Star of the Week'.
I feel cheerful when I play with my dog.
I feel very happy when my mum buys me sweets.
I feel very glad when I go to a party.
I feel cheerful when I eat chocolate.

Joanna Bailie (8)
The Diamond Primary School

White Cow, White Cow

(Inspired by 'Baa Baa Black Sheep')

'White cow, white cow,
Have you any milk?'
'Sorry Sir, sorry Sir,
Only cans of Lilt.
One for my brother,
One for my sister,
And one for her little friend
Who has a very sore blister.'

Adam Kirk & Richard Gibson (11)
The Diamond Primary School

Farming

F is for Friesian cows,
A is for all the animals,
R is for red hens clucking,
M is for milking parlour,
I is for into the fields we run,
N is for never play near machinery,
G is for always close the gates.

Winston Logan (8)
The Diamond Primary School

Feeling Happy

I feel happy when I play with my friends.
I feel excited on Saturdays when I go to the farm.
I feel glad when my friends come to my house.
I feel cheerful when I play hide-and-seek with my friends.

David Fenton (7)
The Diamond Primary School

To Spar, To Spar

(Inspired by 'To Market, To Market')

To Spar, to Spar,
To buy a brown loaf.
Home again, home again,
Two slices of toast.
To Spar, to Spar,
To buy some ham.
Home again, home again,
Put on the pan.

Andrew Lyness & Adam Balmer (10)
The Diamond Primary School

Pat, Pat

(Inspired by 'Tom, Tom, the Piper's Son')

Pat, Pat, the farmer's son,
Stole a pig and away did run,
The cow was lost and Pat was cross
And Pat went crying to the moss.

Lisa Rutherford & Faith Graham (11)
The Diamond Primary School

Old Fat Brad

(Inspired by 'Old King Cole')

Old Fat Brad
Was a merry old lad
And a merry old lad was he.
He called for his dog,
And he called for his cat,
And he called for his chickens three.

Sam Linton & Dale Hamilton (10)
The Diamond Primary School

Polly, Polly

(Inspired by 'Mary, Mary Quite Contrary')

Polly, Polly, had a dolly,
How do you groom her hair?
With ribbons and bows
And bobbles that glow.

Kirsty McClintock (10)
The Diamond Primary School

There Was An Old Man

(Inspired by 'There was an Old Woman Who Lived in a Shoe')

There was an old man who lived with a donkey,
He played so much music and became very funky.
When he was finished, he was all worn out,
So he got into bed and turned out the light.

Reuben Bailie (9) & Lee Millar (10)
The Diamond Primary School

Sing A Rap

(Inspired by 'Sing a Song of Sixpence')

Sing a rap for 50 pence,
A pocket full of change,
Lots of sweets in the shop,
All within our range!

Paul Kerr (9) & Gareth Workman (10)
The Diamond Primary School

What Is White?

White are the clouds in the sky.
White are the snowflakes falling.
White are the flowers growing in spring.
White is fresh new milk.
White is slippery ice on the ground.
White is the teacher writing on the board.
White is a fluffy sheep.
White are footsteps in the snow . . .

Hannah Kirk (9) & Janelle McCloy (10)
The Diamond Primary School

What Is White?

As cuddly as baby penguins playing in the snow,
As cute as Arctic foxes running on the ice,
As fluffy as baby polar bears fighting,
As small as a Scottie dog,
As cold as snow blowing in your face.

Catherine Watson (8) & Erinn Byrne (9)
The Diamond Primary School

Morning

Ring, ring, goes the clock,
Woof, woof, goes the dog.
Birds cheeping.
Pop goes the toast!
Pitter-patter goes the rain.
Cars - *beep, beep!*
Cows mooing,
Kettle whistling,
The teachers says, 'Good morning.'

Sophie Peacock (9)
The Diamond Primary School

Simple Simon

(Inspired by 'Simple Simon')

Simple Simon met a butcher
Going to the lake,
Says Simple Simon to the butcher,
'Let me taste your steak.'

David Simpson (9) & Jonathan Jordan (10)
The Diamond Primary School

Paula, Paula

(Inspired by 'Tom, Tom, the Piper's Son')

Paula, Paula, the vicar's daughter
Was sent to church to marry a doctor.
The vows were said, the Bible was read,
They got the rings from the best man, Fred.

Adele McFetridge (11)
The Diamond Primary School

Animal Acrostic

F unny little fish
I n the tank,
S wimming about,
H aving fun.

Trevor Holmes (9)
The Diamond Primary School